In the Province of the Dragon

Sophie Sackville Newton, circa 1890

In the Province of the Dragon

A Pioneer Deaconess in Southern China from
the Boxer Uprising to the Communist Insurgency

Robert *and* Linda Banks

☙PICKWICK *Publications* • Eugene, Oregon

IN THE PROVINCE OF THE DRAGON
A Pioneer Deaconess in Southern China
from the Boxer Uprising to the Communist Insurgency

Copyright © 2025 Robert Banks and Linda Banks. All rights reserved. Except for brief quotations in critical publications or reviews, no part of this book may be reproduced in any manner without prior written permission from the publisher. Write: Permissions, Wipf and Stock Publishers, 199 W. 8th Ave., Suite 3, Eugene, OR 97401.

Pickwick Publications
An Imprint of Wipf and Stock Publishers
199 W. 8th Ave., Suite 3
Eugene, OR 97401

www.wipfandstock.com

PAPERBACK ISBN: 979-8-3852-2967-3
HARDCOVER ISBN: 979-8-3852-2968-0
EBOOK ISBN: 979-8-3852-2969-7

Cataloguing-in-Publication data:

Names: Banks, Robert, author. | Banks, Linda, author.

Title: In the province of the dragon : a pioneer deaconess in southern China from the boxer uprising to the communist insurgency / by Robert and Linda Banks.

Description: Eugene, OR: Pickwick Publications, 2025. | Includes bibliographical references.

Identifiers: ISBN 979-8-3852-2967-3 (paperback). | ISBN 979-8-3852-2968-0 (hardcover). | ISBN 979-8-3852-2969-7 (ebook).

Subjects: LCSH: Biography—Missionaries. | China—Missions. | Missionaries—Australia—Biography.

Classification: BR1288 B360 2025 (print). | BR1288 (ebook).

VERSION NUMBER 02/04/25

A shorter, preliminary, version of this book for an Australian audience was published as *View from the Faraway Pagoda*, by Acorn Press Ltd, Sydney, Australia, 2013. ABN 50 008 549 540.

Unless otherwise indicated, Scripture quotations are taken from the Holy Bible, New International Version © 1973, 1978 by the International Bible Society, used by permission of Zondervan Bible Publishers.

To single female servants of God
who have risked all for the sake of Christ.

Contents

List of Figures | viii
Sources of Figures | x
Explanatory Notes | xi
Prelude: Tracking Down the Original Story | xiii

1 A Girl from the Country to a Deaconess in the City | 1
2 A Little Band of Sisters in "No-Man's" Land | 21
3 Chinese Whispers and Witness in the Fading Middle Kingdom | 40
4 Striving for Reform as the "Sleeping Dragon" Awakes | 58
5 A New Republic stirs up the Winds of Change | 76
6 Recalled to Wider Ministry in the City of Banyan Trees | 94
7 Passing on the Lantern and Honored by the Community | 111
8 Missing Her Adopted Land and Longing for a Heavenly Home | 130

Postlude: Becoming Part of the Ongoing Story | 147
Bibliography | 151

Figures

01 Frontispiece: Sophie Sackville Newton, circa 1890 | ii
02 Sophie's parents, John and Emma Newton | 2
03 Locations in NSW where the Newtons lived | 4
04 "Cambridge Terrace," Newtown, Sydney | 8
05 Sophie in deaconess uniform, with Amy, Grace and Florence | 13
06 Robert Stewart, his wife and co-workers, killed in Kucheng | 17
07 Nantai Island: CMS School bottom left | 22
08 Bridge of Ten Thousand Ages on the Min River | 25
09 View over Nantai Island to the Old City of Foochow | 26
10 Places Sophie served during her years in Fukien | 31
11 Faraway Pagoda in Lieng Kong District | 35
12 Sophie and the Girls School choir in Deng-doi | 39
13 Minna, Sophie and Amy with a Women's School class, 1899 | 41
14 Women missionaries' house at Deng-doi | 43
15 Photos taken at the height of the Boxer Rebellion | 45
16 View over Kuliang in mountains near Foochow | 57
17 An example of the horrific consequences of foot-binding | 62
18 Anti-opium League public meeting un Lieng Kong | 63
19 Typical "baby tower" in rural Fukien | 65
20 Sample page from Sophie's journal 1908–1910 | 68

FIGURES

21 Imposing West Gate in city of Lieng Kong | 73
22 Hospital and dispensary in Lieng Kong mission | 78
23 Decorated entrance of Lieng Kong mission compound | 81
24 The Blind Boys School Band in uniform | 85
25 Bishop John Hind | 89
26 CMS Girls School on Nantai Island | 95
27 Sophie's study at the CMS Girls School in Foochow | 96
28 Breakfast on the verandah in Kuliang | 98
29 Missionary outing on way to the Moon Temple | 99
30 The word "deaconess" in Chinese characters | 102
31 A copy of Sophie's passport | 108
32 Students at Girls Boarding School in Lieng Kong City | 114
33 Deaconess Ding Sieu-Giong (2nd from left, back row) with her six sisters | 120
34 Sophie's mobile chair that she took on her longer trips | 123
35 Letter from Sophie reported in *The Church Missionary Gleaner* | 125
36 Original Chinese version of the letter from Lieng Kong Church to CMS | 128
37 St Paul's Anglican Church, Woodford, in the 1930s | 132
38 A copy of the Coronation program | 134
39 Archbishop Howard and Mrs. Dorothy Mowll on overseas trip | 137
40 Deaconess Reunion—Sophie in front row, 3rd from left | 141
41 The last photograph of Sophie, aged 90 | 145
    Postlude: Ancient Banyan Tree on Nantai Island, Foochow | ?

Sources of Figures

We would like to acknowledge the following sources for allowing us to reproduce their figures with permission:

- Banks Family Collection (Frontispiece, 01, 02, 03, 04, 05, 10, 11, 20. 26, 27, 28, 29, 30, 31, 36, 41, Postlude).
- James Bell Family Collection © 2012 (34).
- Centre for the History of Christian Thought, Sydney (37, 39).
- Church Missionary Society, Australia (01,13, 24. 35, 40).
- Church Missionary Society, United Kingdom (08, 14, 18, 21, 22, 23, 26, 33).
- Other sources are in the Public Domain (06, 07, 09, 15, 17, 19, 21, 25, 38).

Explanatory Notes

- Sections in each chapter are demarcated by the Chinese characters for "Sophie" 梁劉柔芬.
- Original forms of distance measurement rather than metric have been used in the text and preserved in quotations.
- To preserve historical atmosphere, and original spelling of references in quotes from primary sources, older spelling of place names in China has been retained:

Amoy (Xiamen)

Deng-doi (Dongdaichen)

Foochow (Fuzhou)

Formosa (Taiwan)

Fukien (Fujian)

Kuliang (Guling)

Lieng Kong City (Fencheng)

Lieng Kong District (Liangjang)

Nanking (Nanjing)

Peking (Beijing)

Szechwan (Sichuan)

Prelude

Tracking Down the Original Story

STORIES SOMETIMES TAKE A long time to come together. This is one of them. It began by Robert learning that his ageing grandaunt, Sophie Sackville Newton, had spent most of her life in China. Since, after her return to Australia, she lived in the mountains some distance away, as a young child he had no contact with her. Partly because she had picked up a few Chinese traits, and had a strong Christian commitment, she was also regarded as a little exotic by the wider family. They usually referred to her as "China Auntie."

He did not meet her until his mid-teens. By then, she had moved to a missionary retirement home in the city where he lived. During his first year at university, she asked to meet him. Greeting him with a wide smile, and ushering him into a comfortable lounge room, over tea and scones she engaged him warmly in conversation. Though now in her early nineties, she was still lively and eager to find out about his interests, studies, and attitude to Christianity. In fact, she was more concerned to talk about these than her own life and work. Since by then Robert had a genuinely personal faith, and was strongly involved in his local church, there was plenty to discuss. At the end of their time together, she asked if they could kneel so she could pray for him. The time with her left a very vivid impression.

Sophie died in the middle of the following year. To his surprise, Robert found that in her will she had left him most of her personal documents and devotional books. These included several closely-written journals, a prayer diary, a number of circular letters, two passports, and a few family photos. As well, there were two fragmentary autobiographical accounts, outlines of talks she had given and, in the margins of a Bible and Prayer Book references to significant people and events in her life. Along with a collection of overseas postcards, mainly of England and Israel, there was a handwritten booklet with photos taken in China for nephews and nieces, a commendatory letter from her church in China, and a small portion of an ancient Jewish scroll. Knowing Robert's interest in and study of history, Sophie had decided to leave these materials to him in the hope that one day he might write up her story.

When, after graduating from Theological College, he sought to find out more about his grandaunt's work he encountered various obstacles. Unfortuately, many of her regular reports to the local branch of the Church Missionary Society had been destroyed in a fire. Since her annual letters to its headquarters in the UK were only available in London, it was not until he was pursuing doctoral study several years later that he was able to consult them. Even then, a fifty-year privacy rule restricted his reading to her earlier letters and, since there were no photocopying facilities, making copies of these slowly by hand. While studying in Cambridge, he was also able to visit the nearby village of Isleham where his grandaunt was born, as well as other locations associated with forbears who migrated from England to Australia.

Disappointingly, the material Sophie left behind covered only portions of her life, and information he had gathered only filled in certain details. Over the following years, based in Australia, Robert was unable to make much headway in writing up her story. He did, hoever, confirm a link, unknown to the wider family, she mentioned about one of Australia's most famous early explorers being her uncle. He was also able to interview a later China missionary who had regular contact with Sophie during her final years in Australia. Along the way, he discovered that one of her distant nieces also had a few of her personal papers and artifacts that she was willing to share.

Towards the end of the 1990s, the way opened up to find out more of Sophie's story. He and Linda learned that the Australian National Library had purchased some of the key UK Church Missionary Society archives. She also discovered that the its recently digitalised Australian newspaper collection unexpectedly contained over one hundred items about Sophie's talks and activities during her furloughs in various parts of the State. Though some of these were brief, others were full-length records of what

PRELUDE: TRACKING DOWN THE ORIGINAL STORY

she said or did. These two sets of materials began to fill in many of the gaps, and provide a range of broader perspectives, in her story.

In the meantime, we were able to make contact with several senior missionaries and more distant family who shared stories about her later years. New research and publications on the recent history of Christianity in China, including Fujian, and on its wider social, cultural, and political setting, placed her life and work in a broader context. Linda unearthed more archival missionary photos in UK and US university libraries.

Her investigations also located a younger convert in Fuzhou who, with the help of a retired Professor in the city, had developed a blog sharing stories and photos of earlier missionary activities in Fujian province. In the early 2010s, together with a young woman who had completed a doctorate in early missionaries there, they helped us make a brief visit to Fujian to visit places where Sophie lived and worked that were still standing though now unused. These included where she stayed after her arrival, the former CMS Girls' school and chapel where she taught, the boundary of the cemetery where remains of those massacred were buried, and the mission church which was her initial base as a deaconess. A representative of the TSPM church took us a two-hour drive north of the city to the now empty mission compound she had earlier helped construct.

When a delegation of church leaders from Fuzhou later visited Sydney, we were invited to be part of the official welcoming group in the St Andrews House, next door to the Anglican Cathedral. This paved the way for returning to Fuzhou twice more over the next few years.

Meanwhile we completed, edited, and published a preliminary account of Sophie's life entitled *View from the Faraway Pagoda* for a general Australian readership. This was launched in early 2013 at the annual Church Missionary Society Summer School near Sydney at which Sophie had spoken just over a century earlier. Its style and format were enhanced by Linda's creative ideas as an educator, though, at points, we had to skate over portions of Sophie's story about which we had less knowledge, and were only able to include a limited number of footnotes and bibliography.

Since then, we have discovered further documents that fill in aspects of her story, consulted scholarly research that heightens her historical significance, visited more sites connected to her work during lengthier visits to Fujian, established links there with people exploring in mission history in the region, met with members of churches where she worked, and were introduced to an elderly woman whose father and aunt Sophie had adopted.

PRELUDE: TRACKING DOWN THE ORIGINAL STORY

As a result, we decided to undertake a full reworking of this earlier account for a thoughtful international audience. This contains new and more detailed information, additional photographs, full footnotes and bibliography.

We have also given it a new title that reflects the centrality of the dragon in Chinese imagination. It was both a key symbol *in* but also *of* China itself. Unlike its depiction in Western culture as a menacing, fire-eating monster, dragons were regarded as wise and benevolent powerful beings that portray courage and adventurousness. Though, for Sophie, going to such a large, distant country as China involved stepping out into the unknown and, given its basic medical and legal facilities, a degree of risk-taking, she did not view it as a dangerous setting, especially given her confidence in God's leading and protection.

All this brings to life more vitally, and does fuller justice to, an unassuming but remarkable Christian woman who devoted her life to the people and country she adopted as her own.

1

A Girl from the Country to a Deaconess in the City

SOPHIE SACKVILLE NEWTON WAS born into a changing world.[1] The year 1867 marked the formation of the Dominion of Canada, Singapore becoming a Crown Colony, a closer linking of East and West through the Suez Canal, and the end of transporting convicts from England to Australia. Family circumstances led to Sophie's birth in far-off England while her father, John, was furthering his medical qualifications, accompanied by his wife Emma, daughter Hannah, and son George. Initially, they rented a cottage in the village of Isleham not far from Cambridge, where Sophie was baptized in the Anglican church.

---

1. Unless otherwise referenced, material on Sophie in this chapter comes from her personal documents in the Banks Family Collection. This opening section is partly drawn from S. Newton, My Early Life, 1–2.

Sophie's parents, John and Emma Newton

The following year, the family moved into the heart of Cambridge, first into a house in Trumpington St where George contracted croup and sadly died. Over the next three years, two more children, Amelia and John, were born. By the early seventies, they were living in a two-storey corner house in Regent St, overlooking a large park on one side and the main route from the railway station into the city center on the other. Sophie's first memories here were of students in flowing black gowns, imposing sandstone Colleges, colorful daily markets in the Town Square, and people punting on the river Cam.

Sophie's parents had married two years after John migrated from England to set up a practice in northern New South Wales (NSW). Australian-born Emma now had the opportunity of meeting his parents, a Methodist minister and his wife, along with his brother William, an Anglican clergyman, and two other siblings.[2] Living in Cambridge near the Hospital, John was now preparing for admission to the prestigious Royal College of Surgeons, and supporting the family through a small practice on the ground floor of their terrace house. Even as a small child, Sophie became used to seeing sick people coming in and out of her home. Early in 1872, Emma fell pregnant again but developed complications that made her fearful of dying in childbirth. They decided to return to Australia so she would have the support of her family, especially as they would have five children under eight years old. It was serendipitous to hear that William and his wife, Catherine, were planning to emigrate to Australia and serve in an Anglican church in the colony of NSW.

The family moved to London for a few months until they could find a steamer heading for Australia that required a ship's doctor to help cover the expenses. During that time, Sophie was shown where Queen Victoria lived, Buckingham Palace, as well as Westminster Abbey, where so many famous British people were buried, and the Tower of London, where others had been wrongfully imprisoned. When the family eventually embarked on the SS *Parramatta*, she enjoyed meeting passengers from several Western cultures and, among the crew, getting her first glimpse of several Chinese, who were wearing a queue, dressed in simple oriental garments, and speaking a very different language.[3] Along with her parents, she was also able to experience sailing through the recently completed Suez Canal. The initial delay in finding a passage meant that Emma gave birth on board—to everyone's relief baby Herbert arrived without complications—shortly before the ship's arrival in Sydney before Christmas.

Over the next couple of months, the Newtons stayed with Emma's widowed mother, Elizabeth, and married brother, at "Stafford," a mixed farm near the country town of Singleton, a hundred and twenty-five miles north-west of Sydney. It was here that Sophie met her Australian grandma, uncle, and aunt, and experienced country life for the first time.

---

2. It was from Rev John's wife, Hannah, nee Sackfield, that Sophie's middle name was derived.

3. See the passenger list for S *Parramatta* at https:/marineships.com.au and information about crews on British ships around this time in Yu Pa-ching, "Chinese Seamen in London and St. Helena in the Nineteenth Century": in Law, Labour and Empire, London: Palgrave MacMillan,287–303 (also at https://doi.org/10.1057/9781137447463_16).

Locations in NSW where the Newtons lived

Before long, John was offered a temporary position in the small country town of Queanbeyan in the southern part of the State, where a younger sister, Grace, was born. In 1874 the family moved north of Sydney again to Mudgee, where John had opened a practice when he first arrived in Australia. This brought them close to his brother William, now Rector of the neighboring town of Gulgong. It did not take long for John to resume his former standing in the town, often appearing in court as a forensic expert and ultimately becoming the district coroner. Sophie, now seven, established a special bond with William's daughter Eleanor, who was similar in age. While this move was a welcome one for her parents, a very practical problem soon arose. There was simply not enough room in the house for all six children. In consultation with Emma's family, they decided that the three oldest—Sophie, Hannah, and Amy—would go to live with Uncle Samuel, Aunt Mary and grandmother Elizabeth at "Stafford", where there was both space and household help.

The placing of children in the care of relatives was not unusual at this time, as families thought of themselves in extended rather than just nuclear terms. Since "Stafford" was where Sophie's mother had grown up, it was a place where the girls felt at home and could easily be visited by their parents. It was here she learned to cook, garden, and play the piano, as well as how to ride a horse, and help out with harvesting crops. Sophie gained a great deal from her aunt and grandmother who modeled independence and resilience in helping to manage a large property, and dealing with the challenges and vicissitudes of life on the land.[4]

The three sisters attended the public school and local church in the small village of Warkworth a few miles away. This was part of a very scattered parish where members often had to meet in homestead churches. Apart from these activities, there were occasional trips in horse and cart with the family to the closest major center, Singleton, to shop and attend social events. Less often, Sophie made the longer trip in the other direction to Mudgee to spend time with her family, especially for birthdays and Christmas. Although she had grown up in a Christian family, Sophie's experience of family devotions with her grandma, aunt and sisters at "Stafford" left a lasting impression. They sang and read regularly from a small book of *Hymns for Little Children*, which also contained the Ten Commandments as well as morning and evening prayers. As these times were simply part of their daily routine, she learned that you did not need to go to a special building, or have a special service, to experience God with other people.

During evening meals, and leisurely Sunday afternoons, the children often pleaded with grandma to tell them about favorite family stories. This was how Sophie heard about James Kennedy and his eight years old daughter, the first to migrate from England only a few years after Australia was settled. His sister, Eliza, was the first woman appointed by the Governor to found and direct the new colony's Girls Orphanage. Sophie's great grandfather John Howe, had opened up a way north through largely inhospitable terrain from Sydney to Singleton. Grandma's husband, George Dight, who died unexpectedly in his late forties, was elected as a member of the first Parliament. A famous uncle, Hamilton Hume, had with aboriginal help discovered a workable overland route from Sydney to Australia's southern coast.[5] The lives of these adventurous, sometimes risk-taking pioneers who helped build the fledging society, left a lasting impression on teenage Sophie.

In April 1876, the girls received a letter from their parents to say that she had a new little sister, Florence. Life went on without incident for the next few years until three weeks before Christmas 1880, when Sophie's older

---

4. A fascinating evocation of everyday life in the country in this period may be found in M. Franklin, *Childhood at Brindabella* and, on a broader scale by Blainey, *Black Kettle and Full Moon*.

5. See further Arndell, *Pioneers of Portland Head*; "John Howe," ADB, vol.1; "Eliza More Kennedy," ADEB, 176–7; "John Dight and his Descendants," RRHSQ, 10–20; and Manne, *Hamilton Hume*, respectively.

sister Hannah died unexpectedly of rheumatic fever. Hannah's death was heart-wrenching for her parents, as a deeply grieving letter from her father to his mother-in-law Elizabeth shows. Recalling their loss of son George ten years earlier, he took comfort from the fact that "our eldest girl and boy are in heaven", John and Emma had now lost two children, and again Sophie had to face the death of someone very close to her.[6] Coupled with this, she now felt the pressure and responsibility of being the eldest child.

During these teenage years, Sophie's personal faith continued to develop. Around the age of seventeen, she began reading a widely used devotional booklet *Daily Light*, a practice she engaged in throughout her life. Although always regarding herself as a Christian, on 23 July 1885 she was confirmed in the Singleton Anglican church as a sign of her wholehearted commitment to Christ.

梁劉柔芬

Shortly after she turned nineteen, an age when many young women were becoming engaged or married, Sophie took up employment as a governess. This position involved responsibility for seven younger cousins at "Boonal," an expansive cattle and sheep station in the far north of NSW owned by her uncle George and aunt Isabella. Her responsibility was chiefly to broaden and improve the children's reading, writing, and musical skills, which developed her teaching for a quite diverse age range. This first experience of earning a living also taught Sophie how to be thrifty. In addition to lessons with each of the children, she was inevitably involved with the many aspects of life on a large, remote property and its ever-changing seasons.

During her two-year stay at "Boonal," Sophie received letters from her sisters in Singleton. Their correspondence contains strong indications of their mutual faith in God and prayers for one another.[7] It also reveals Sophie's growing spiritual commitment, that was captured in a poem she copied out at that time:

> ... Ask of Me
> That strength that thou
> Dost not possess,
> But which in all thy weakness shall be perfect made

6. John Newton, Letter to his mother, 12 December 1880.

7. Letters from Grace Newton, July 1887, and from Florence Newton, December 1887.

If only thou wilt find thy source in Me!" . . .
"Yes. Lord!", I cried,
"So place the burden that I may leave
With all my weight on Thee,
Nor keep the load myself
And I will walk close by Thy side,
Nor fear the journey if Thou shalt lead me.[8]

Towards the end of the following year, Sophie moved back to Mudgee when her aunt Isabella's seriously declining health led to the property being put up for sale. Back home, she was pursued by an eligible young man in the district, whose father was a well-known wealthy grazier and businessman. It is not clear how long they kept company, but the relationship was close enough for him to propose marriage and for her to accept. However, Sophie began to have second thoughts and painfully ended the relationship. She sensed that God was drawing her towards a different life than that of a wife and mother, and needed to wait for Him to reveal where that might lead.

---

8. From *The Master's Message*, author and provenance unknown.

"Cambridge Terrace," Newtown, Sydney

In early 1891, a new opportunity opened up for the entire family. John decided to begin a medical practice not far from the recently established Royal Prince Alfred Hospital in Sydney, which would open the door to part-time consultancy and teaching there. The family moved into a comfortable terrace house just down from the Hospital and nearby University. Their home was adjacent to a working-class district and it was among low-paid and sometimes unemployed people, that his practice served.

Relocation from the country to the city provided the older siblings with greater work possibilities and brought them closer to their uncle William who had been invited to become Principal of St Philip's Grammar School in the city. For Sophie, the move to the colony's capital was a good one, as it gave her a fresh start after a broken engagement. While looking for work, she found various ways of serving at her local, evangelical, Anglican church, St Barnabas, Broadway.[9] The young Rector, Rev Martin, encouraged her to be involved in evangelism, pastoral visiting, and its growing Sunday School. Later that year, a well-known Irish missioner, George Grubb, and his team came to Australia to conduct interdenominational conventions in Australia. In October, one of these was held at St Barnabas. Its focus was a deeper knowledge of the spiritual life, a greater reliance on the Holy Spirit for growth and witness, and a commitment to the evangelization of the world. These interdenominational meetings had their roots in the annual Keswick Week in England's picturesque Lake District, to which people came from all over the country.

From the moment she heard about the Convention, Sophie became involved in door-to-door visitation to promote it. During the week-long event, she hardly missed a meeting. Grubb was a charismatic speaker, and his addresses were full of strong emotion, humorous asides, and contemporary analogies. An illustration he often used was of God having a phonograph recording every word we speak, and of us one day standing before Him hearing again not only our words but the tone in which we uttered them. Towards the end of the convention, he gave an hour-long talk titled "The Beginning of Months." This was based on God's word to Moses in Exodus 12:2: "This month shall mark for you the beginning of months; it shall be the first month of the year for you."[10]

Although Sophie knew she was a Christian, Grubb's invitation helped her overcome an occasional lack of full confidence in this. As she wrote later, "I can never forget how gladly I surrendered all that night, 10pm, when given the opportunity to testify, assurance of salvation, call to life

---

9. The character and influence of evangelicalism in Sydney, and elsewhere in Australia, at this time is admirably summarized in Piggin and Linder, *Fountain of Public Prosperity: Evangelical Christians in Australian History 1870–1914*, Melbourne: Monash University Press, 2018, 493–520.

10. A brief account of Grubb's Mission may be found in Chant, *Beyond Protestantism*, 180–182, and thoroughly in Millard, *The Same Lord*.

service, and the mission field ... Many were greatly blessed and rose up and followed ... My own great longing was to go straight into full-time service for the Master, but my father died very soon after and I had to seek some means of helping my family."[11]

John died of unexpected medical complications from appendicitis shortly after Christmas. He was just 53. When Sophie opened his desk to sort through his affairs, they found a desk full of accounts he had been too soft-hearted to send out. As a result, the family was practically penniless. The volume of outstanding accounts in his largely working-class practice was overwhelming, and John was too soft-hearted to press for payment if people were experiencing hardship. As the eldest child, Sophie felt responsible to help financially support her grieving mother and five younger siblings. Within the month, the Newtons had moved out of their terrace to cheaper premises in the adjacent inner city suburb of Glebe.

梁劉柔芬

Despite continued efforts, a deepening economic depression in Australia prevented Sophie from finding work.[12] In desperation she cried out to God, recording that:

> God very definitely led me to Psalm 37:3–5.
>
> Trust in the Lord,
> and do good;
> so shalt thou dwell in the Land,
> and verily thou shalt be fed.
> Delight thyself also in the Lord:
> and he shall give thee
> the desires of thine heart.
> Commit thy way unto the Lord;
> trust also in him:
> And he shall bring it to pass," (KJV)[13]

---

11. This, and the following, quote, comes from S. S. Newton, How I became a Deaconess, 1.

12. The extensive effects of this Depression are explored in, Crowley, *History of Australia*, Melbourne: Heinemann, 1977, ch.5, and more extensively in Bolton, *A Fine Country*, Perth: University of Western Australia, 1974. Stannage, C.T.

13. S. S. Newton, How I became a Deaconess, 2.

From this she realized that though God knew her deepest desire was to serve him, she could trust him to fulfil this in the future. In the meantime, her priority was to find work that would financially support the family.

A few weeks later, as she was praying, one of only three deaconesses in Sydney Anglican churches came to mind, and Sophie thought that this kind of work would be ideal. The following Sunday, after church she found herself talking with that same deaconess about her work of visiting the sick and poor.[14]

> [I] remarked how I longed to do the same, but added that God had given me His word and that I was content. And now the wonderful thing happened. On the following Tuesday I had been out, and on my return I found a strange clergyman in the dining room (though I had seen him at the Mission). I told him Mother would soon be home but he replied: "I came to see you. I have come to ask if you will be my deaconess." I could only say: "I must ask the Lord."[15]

They went out onto the balcony and the clergyman, Rev Mullens, pointed out his inner-city parish in Pyrmont, and arranged for Sophie and her mother to look at the church and meet his wife later in the week. This led to Sophie accepting his offer. Her wages included board and lodging at the Rectory along with a salary of £80 a year. This enabled the family to rent a small cottage not far from St Bartholomew's church. Renting this modest dwelling consumed most of Sophie's stipend, until her two younger siblings found work and could help financially.

Deaconesses had been introduced into the Church of England several decades earlier to provide care for desperate families in the sprawling industrial suburbs. When serious economic depression took hold in Australia in the 1890s, it became crucial for the church to engage in both social as well as pastoral outreach to poverty-stricken families, especially in inner-city slums. These families faced unemployment at a time where there was no safety net, government pension plan, or universal health cover. The situation was exacerbated by the growing numbers of middle-class people leaving from the inner city to less crowded suburbs. The socially conscious churches like Broadway and Pyrmont were at the forefront of grappling with these issues.

---

14. Further on this subject, see Nora Tess, *Caught for Life: The Story of the Anglican Deaconess Order in Australia*, Araluen, 1993, self-published, especially 21ff.

15. S. S. Newton, How I became a Deaconess, 2.

Although feeling, untrained and inexperienced, especially in an area full of slums and factories, Sophie found Rev Mullens wise, loving, and humble. Instead of curbing what she regarded as rashness, he discerningly channeled her enthusiasm into regular women's and prayer groups, as well as assisting him in weekly open-air and lunch-hour meetings. The latter took some courage, as they were held among male and female employees at the nearby saw and sugar mills. Before making pastoral visits, the two met together for consultation, sharing, and prayer over every house call. At the end of this time of practical training, on 6 November 1892 Archbishop Saumarez Smith ordained her as a deaconess. Since all three previous deaconesses had come from overseas as adults, Sophie was the first to be raised, educated, and trained in Australia. For her, being the first "home-grown" deaconess was a special honor.

Sophie in uniform, with Amy, Grace, and Florence

During 1892, Sophie's horizons continued to expand through the opportunities she was given at Pyrmont. These were broadened dramatically as a result of hearing a British Church Missionary Society [CMS] speaker, Rev Robert Stewart, from Fukien Province in China, who was accompanied by Dr Eugene Stock, the Society's Secretary. In his address, Robert Stewart began by talking about China as a wonderful country that was civilized long before the West and contained great natural resources.

Its people had been educated since the time of Confucius, five hundred years before Christ, and he had taught many valuable things about personal and family behavior. In China, it was important to learn a number of these rules, as otherwise the people would view foreigners as uneducated barbarians and not listen to them.

Stewart went on to explain that the Chinese had three main religions—Confucianism, Buddhism, and Taoism—but that for individuals Buddhism was the most important. The latter's weakness was that its answer to the trials and tribulations of life was the eradication of desire. And so, since ordinary people found this impossible to achieve, they succumbed to the lure of idols. Though they knew these were made of wood, devotees believed a spirit existed within them. The speaker held up the kind of graven figure that families in every Chinese house prayed to for protection and a tiny shoe that was used to cruelly bind and deform the feet of infant girls. He also talked about so-called "baby towers" outside cities with a small slot into which new-born baby girls were frequently abandoned.

While there were now nearly a hundred thousand believers in China, Stewart said, there was still only one missionary for every quarter of a million people. Most of these were women, and through these, some Chinese pastors, catechists, and bible women, God was working. The strategy was to establish day schools, where even girls could now be educated, as well as hear stories and sing hymns about Jesus. There were also new medical centers, which brought healing to countless sick people with the opportunity to hear the gospel and see it in action. There was, however, a cost involved in serving in a strange, occasionally violent, country. He encouraged his audience to ask if God was calling them to help build the house He was constructing in China, to wait patiently for an answer and, if it came, to not hold back.[16]

An important outcome of Stewart and Stock's visit was the restructuring of the Anglican mission societies in the Australian colonies that to this point were merely branches of the British CMS. These now became semi-autonomous, described themselves as Church Missionary Associations (CMA) rather than just Auxiliaries, and were able to select their own candidates as well as decide where to send them. The first to do this were those based in New South Wales and Victoria (which also included

---

16. Stewart's addresses were widely reported in Sydney and Melbourne newspapers, but often more extensively in major country centers he visited, such as the *Goulburn Evening Penny Press*, 20 September 1892, 4, from which most of the above is drawn.

Tasmania). As a result of Stewart's impact, these decided to make China their primary focus. Four years later, the separate Church of England Zenana Mission, which recruited only women, some of whom were already in China, merged with CMA Victoria.

The first to take up Stewart's challenge were two young sisters, Eleanor and Elizabeth Saunders, from the neighboring colony of Victoria, who were accepted by its Church Missionary Association (CMA), and were invited by Stewart to join the CMS mission station at Kucheng in the interior of Fukien. Sophie had the opportunity to meet them when their ship berthed for a few days in Sydney en route to China. Although she would have liked to follow them as soon as possible, it was clear that family responsibilities required her to wait for a time. She needed to help other members of the family find employment. Though the continuing downturn in the economy made this difficult, Sophie was able to arrange for one of her brothers to train in dentistry and two of her sisters in nursing.

In 1894, Rev Moreton, a strong supporter of the NSW CMAssociation, invited her to gain further deaconess experience at his very mission-minded church of St Luke's Burwood.[17] Although this was a more middle-class parish, Sophie was given responsibility for the almost completely unchurched, working-class end of the suburb. She began by visiting a large number of homes to invite children to a new Sunday School she was starting. This met in a cottage close to a large factory, but was so successful that it quickly outgrew the premises and moved to a rented hall nearby. As a result of her work, a number of the parents became interested in Christianity and joined the church.

According to the parish's 150th *Anniversary History*, Sophie

> reported to Parish Council that people in this area needed their own church as it was too far to go to St Luke's. Her success in building the congregation persuaded Mrs Starling of Park Road, Burwood, to endow £439 —enough to buy the Queen Street site and to build the original section of St Peter's Mission Church [which] was opened in 1896.[18]

While she was helping this new congregation to grow, Sophie took every opportunity to prepare herself for China. She read copies of *The Church Missionary Gleaner* magazine when they arrived from England and prayed

---

17. On this church, see further *Between Two Highways*, Sydney: Wentworth, 1969, 64-65.

18. In the St Luke's Burwood magazine, *Prescription*, 18 October 2009, 22-23.

regularly for the Australians who had joined the Stewarts in Kucheng. Borrowing books from the local public library gave her a better appreciation of the history, geography, and culture of the so-called "Middle Kingdom." She made regular visits to her uncle William's parish in Botany, home to the largest number of Chinese Christians in the city. When it was possible, she also spent time with a distant relative, Amy Oxley, who, as a result of Stewart's visit, was preparing to join the mission in Kucheng but delayed by Japan's blockade of Foochow in the war it had started with China.

梁劉柔芬

Opening the main Sydney newspaper on a Wednesday morning in early August 1895, Sophie was shocked to read about a massacre of ten missionaries and a child on Flower Mountain, above the village of Hwasang, in Fukien Province. Among those murdered were Robert and Louisa Stewart and one of their children; sisters Eleanor and Elizabeth Saunders from Melbourne, Annie Gordon from Queensland, and four other women. According to *The Sydney Morning Herald*, the incident involved "Revolting Cuelties," "Ladies Hacked to Death," and "Children Impaled by Spears." This took place towards the close of a small annual conference in the hills above the district capital of Kucheng, and was perpetrated by a hundred-strong group of rural men wielding swords, spears, and pitchforks.[19] These were members of a so-called "Vegetarian Society" that was both anti-Western and opposed to the Qing dynasty for their attempts to overturn traditional Chinese religion and ways, including food habits. In some respects, this group was a precursor of the Boxer Movement that developed and surfaced in northern and inland Chinq over the next few years.

Over the following days, further cables from China provided more detail, including the subsequent death of another of the Stewart's children. These explained that it was the redeployment of Provincial Government troops to help resist Japan's attack upon coastal cities like Foochow, that enabled the "Vegetarians" to take control of part of the district around Kucheng and set up an unofficial alternative government. Their main targets were government officials, foreign workers and their Chinese assistants, along with Christian missionaries.[20]

19. "Massacre in China," *The Sydney Morning Herald*, 7 August 1895, 1.

20. More detailed and complementary accounts, from ither perspectives, of the lead-up to the massacre, its horrific nature, and legal aftermath, are provided in our books

Robert Stewart, wife, and co-workers, killed in Kucheng

News of the massacre ricocheted around the world. Over the following months, its impact featured regularly in both national and regional newspapers.[21] While most people were sympathetic to missionary work in China, others questioned how well mission societies protected their workers, especially women, and a few criticized the arrogance of spreading Christianity

---

Through the Valley, 10–22, and *Children of the Massacre*, 26–37, as well as briefly in *They Shal See His Face*, 12–13.

21. See especially the comprehensive collection in Welch, *The Flower Mountain Murders*, Parts IV, The Huashan Massacre, at https://openresearch-repository.anu.edu>handle.

in foreign lands. Unexpectedly, it motivated a number of young women for service in Fukien to replace those who had been slain.

Sophie was one of the first to do this. Providentially, by the latter half of 1895, the family was no longer dependent upon her income. She had helped Herb find an apprenticeship in dentistry, and Ken had turned up a job in Melbourne. Her introduction of Amy to a young man was leading toward marriage, and Florence was courting a recent emigrant from South Africa. For the first time in four years, Sophie felt free to act upon God's call to missionary service. After talking with Rev Moreton, she approached NSW local CMA about becoming a candidate.

梁劉柔芬

On 10 January 1896, Sophie formally applied to NSW CMA. Six weeks later, on 20 February, they accepted her. That day, she recorded in her Prayer Book "Psalm 37:4: my heart's desire has been granted." This was the passage God had given to her four years earlier before she became a deaconess. The next step, after finishing up in the parish at the end of the year, was a six-month course of study at the recently established Marsden Training Home in a nearby suburb. She had already visited this several times, partly because Amy Oxley studied there and its founder, Eliza Hassall, was also a distant relative. Courses, taught by Eliza and a few visiting clergy included Bible Study, Church History, Mission Geography, and Christian Evidences, as well as object lessons, music, elementary dispensing, and practical challenges of ministry overseas.[22] Sophie was particularly interested in learning more about the Jewish people as, ever since she heard George Grubb's talks, concern for God's people had become part of her prayer life. The chief deficiency in the Training Home's curriculum, a lack of sufficient anthropological, social, and cultural study of relevant countries, was partly due to a lack of teachers with missionary experience.

Interestingly, around this time a lively debate about China was developing in Australia and elsewhere through a visionary book entitled *National Life and Character: A Forecast* by a local academic and politician, Charles H. Pearson. Its author, whose father was Principal of the CMS College in London, had been a Professor of History in Oxford before settling in

---

22. Welch, "Australian and New Zealand Missionary Training Homes," Working Paper, College of Asia and the Pacific, Australian National University, September 2014, 6–7, at https://openresearch-repository.anu.edu.au.

Australia first at Melbourne University and then as Principal of the nearby Presbyterian Ladies College. His book argued that the European urge to civilize Asia would eventually rebound upon it. In particular, it would stimulate China, which for the last quarter of a century had been developing some industrial, manufacturing, and commercial sectors. Through emigration, the Chinese would eventually dominate development in Asia and, within a century, imperial European countries would lose their colonies, and China would become the foremost economic power in the world. The widespread debate over the book indicates that by the 1890s China was by no means viewed by everyone as a weak, backward nation, even if its recent defeat in the war initiated by the more highly industrialized and militarized Japan, did affect its status.[23]

Unfortunately, shortly before entering the Marsden Home, Sophie was diagnosed with typhoid that was circulating in Sydney at the time. It was several months before she had sufficiently recuperated to begin her training. Since there was now less salary coming in, the family had to move again. Fortunately, a small house behind St Andrew's Cathedral became available. Along with the subjects she studied at the Home, she completed a first-aid course conducted by St John's Ambulance.

It was with great joy that, on 13 October 1896, Sophie received news from NSW CMA of her appointment to Foochow, the capital of Fukien Province.[24] Over the next three months, she had to gradually pack enough personal items for her first six-year term; gather official work and travel documents; write letters to far-flung family, friends, and supporters; and speak at meetings in link country and city churches. In view of the horrific events in China the year before, a priority was trying to allay fears of potential danger. Her sister Amy admired her decision and promised to pray regularly. From Melbourne, Ken wrote to "my darling, old Cis," explaining that "since I do not share your religious convictions it's hard for me to understand your decision, but from your point of view I see that you are making the right decision."[25] The rest of the family celebrated

---

23. See Pearson, *National Life and Character*, and the review of Peter Cain, "China, globalization and the west: A British debate, 1890–1914", *History and Policy*, 3 July 2009, at https://www.historyandpolicy.org/policy-papers/papers/china-globalisation-and-the-west-a-british-debate-1890–1914.

24. Instructions from the Church Missionary Association NSW, 1 October 1896.

25. Letter from James Newton, 16 December 1896.

Christmas together and, three days later, the marriage of her youngest sister Florence, to Percy Dyke.[26]

The evening before her departure, the CMA held a Valedictory Service in the city for Sophie and Isobel Suttor, from Tasmania, who had trained with her at the Marsden Home. The Anglican Primate occupied the chair and the large hall was packed. The two women were given their formal instructions and a farewell exhortation. Finally, according to a city newspaper, "both young ladies gave their testimonies in a simple, straightforward manner ... [and] the service was concluded with a commendatory prayer."[27]

The same day, Sophie received a wistful letter from her grandmother in Singleton, who wished her well despite realizing she might not see her again "this side of heaven."[28] The next morning, families of the two young women and other well-wishers turned up at the wharf to see them embark on the SS *Taiyuan* via Darwin for Hong Kong. This Chinese Navigation Company cargo ship had several passenger berths and its crew came from various Chinese provinces. Since Florence was unwell, she sent her apologies. Emma was understandably emotional and tearful. Amy brought a Bible Sophie had given her several months earlier so that she could write a message in it. On board, there were some brief prayers and a hymn. Finally, it was time for the family to disembark and exchange farewells. As the ship began to pull away from the dock, Amy threaded her way along the wharf to keep pace with it, waving and blowing kisses to her sister for as long as she was in sight.

---

26. Florence Newton is one of the authors' (Robert's) grandmother. Her husband Percy was originally from England, settled for a time in South Africa, and then migrated to Australia.

27. *The Daily Telegraph*, 6 January 1897, 6.

28. Letter from Elizabeth Dight, 6 January 1897.

2

A Little Band of Sisters in "No-Man's" Land

THE SS *TAIYUAN* STEAMED out of the harbor Mark Twain had described as "superbly beautiful . . . the darling of Sydney, and . . . wonder of the world", for which one should give "praise to God."[1] Five days later, the ship called in at Brisbane, then worked its way up the Queensland coast, around Cape York, and westwards along the top of Arnhem Land to Darwin. Then it turned north around the tip of New Guinea, finally reaching Hong Kong on 28 January 1897. Sophie and Isobel were hosted by Australian missionaries Rev E Judd Barnett and his wife, local representatives of the CMS. Staying in the British section of the island meant that they had limited contact with Chinese people, but even this piqued their interest in what was to come.

A week later they were on their way again in a smaller boat to Foochow, a four-day trip further north. Their route went up through the South China Sea, calling at several ports on the way, the best known of which was Amoy. Here Sophie caught her first glimpse of China's rocky coastline, featuring numerous inlets, promontories, and small islands. Across the straits to the south-east lay Formosa, which had been occupied by the Japanese in the recent war. After reaching the estuary of the Min River, the chief transport route Fukien Province, the boat made for the main channel. As it sailed upriver towards the capital, on 8 February Sophie climbed on the deck to take in all the sights around her. Since it was mid-winter, with a brisk breeze on the river, she donned her warmest clothes. Misty-covered

---

1. This took place during his visit a year earlier as his book *Mark Twain in Australia*, 112–13, records.

high mountains on either side were criss-crossed by terraces. Every so often the ship passed by a waterfront village, and dozens of junks and sampans were moving up and down the Min. Around twenty miles upstream from the capital, the ship came to rest at Pagoda Anchorage, which was as far as ocean-going vessels could proceed.[2]

Transferring to a sampan for the final few miles of the journey, they neared the city of Foochow shortly after dark. There:

> ... we heard Miss Oxley's voice ... who gave us a real Australian welcome, afterwards seeing us into our rickshaws bidding us not to be afraid. At the same time, I had to admit that I was very glad when we were safely deposited at the Theological College House. It is impossible to describe my joy and satisfaction at being permitted to come to this land after waiting five years.[3]

Nantai Island: CMS School bottom left

---

2. Vivid descriptions of life along the river, and roads leading into Fuhkien, are contained in Dukes, *Everyday Life in China*.

3. S. S. Newton, Annual Letter, 1 December 1897, 1.

A LITTLE BAND OF SISTERS IN "NO-MAN'S" LAND

Theological College House, where she would be staying for the first couple of months was the home of the widowed Principal, Rev John Martin, his two young children, and an amah. Sophie enjoyed the atmosphere of meeting Chinese students and developed a special bond with five-year old Dorothy. Little did she know that the little girl, who loved to sit on her knees, would one day not only become a missionary in China but the wife of a future Archbishop of Sydney and a close friend.[4]

During her first few months, Sophie found everything "very strange and new."[5] Her first task was to learn the local language. This was the Foochow dialect, a form of Hokkien spoken in the capital and its nearby districts. She met with her language teacher for five hours a day, leaving little time for anything else. Aiding her learning was a version of the Bible in the local dialect, which had been completed just five years earlier. *The Book of Common Prayer*, used by Sophie devotionally as well as in church, had also been translated into Fukienese. Sometimes, lessons with her instructor had a quite humorous side. For example, one day, when it was extremely warm, he suddenly stood up and instead of fanning himself began to vigorously fan the wooden chair, as he thought it was getting too hot![6] Fortunately, Sophie soon discovered an aptitude for language learning

She also learned more about the wider history of Christian work in the province. This had begun in 1864, twenty years after the first Protestant missionaries reached China. In its early years there were significant hurdles, including the deaths of its first three representatives. After growing hostility to foreigners owning property in the Old City, in 1876 a portion of land across the Min River on Nantai Island, much of it a cemetery, was granted to American Methodists and then Anglicans, for residences and other buildings. It was not until the 1880s that Christian work took root in the nearby district of Lieng Kong, through the work of a Chinese evangelist. Among Anglicans, the work was divided into districts, each of which had a Senior Missionary, Chinese pastor, and catechist. In the whole province, there were only sixteen Anglican missionaries, eleven clergy, two appointed lay assistants, and three female teachers, along with a number of Chinese

---

4. The story of Sophie "dangling Dorothy on her knee" came down both through the family and friends.

5. S. Newton, Annual Letter, 1 December 1897, 1–2.

6. As told by Miss Suttor and reported in the *Mudgee Guardian and North-western Representative*, 21 October 1909, 18, many years later.

bible-women. There were presently three thousand publicly dedicated Christians, along with several thousand church attenders.[7]

By early March, the cold weather of winter was gradually turning into the warm season that ran until June. Apart from attending St John's Anglican Church on Sundays, and spending time occasionally with other missionaries, Sophie only had time for a little hospital visiting and exploring the area where she was living. This end of Nantai Island was originally the city cemetery and avoided by locals who believed it was inhabited by ghosts. When land had to be found for foreigners, this was regarded by the Chinese as the best option. Not far from the Theological College stood the International Cemetery, where the Kucheng martyrs were buried. The proximity of this final resting place of the Saunders sisters, with its marble angel monument, was an ever-present reminder of the cost of missionary service.[8] The western end of Nantai Island was largely a foreign enclave, separated from the walled city by the ancient Bridge of Ten Thousand Ages. In the foreign concession area, there were many fine English-style buildings, some decorated with Chinese features. Along with the four other mission compounds, it housed two churches, a college, a hospital, the British and American consulates, and a few schools. There were also residences for government officials and business people. Large banyan trees lined some streets, as well as a hill surrounded by patches of lush vegetation. On Sundays, Sophie attended St John's Anglican Church, where the English-language service was led by Rev Lloyd and sometimes Archdeacon John Wolfe, the founder of CMS work in the province. In addition, a Chinese service held at Trinity Theological College helped improve her understanding of the language. During this time, she began to meet members of other missions working in the province, especially those from the two next largest missions, the Methodist (linked with the American Methodist Episcopal Church) and Congregational (under the American Board of Foreign Missions).[9]

---

7. Cole, *Church Missionary Society in Australia* 140–46.

8. Details of the victims' burial and funeral eighteen months earlier, as well as memorial services overseas, are contained in Banks and Banks, *Children of the Massacre*, 33–35.

9. The development of these at this time is discussed by Dunch, *Fuzhou Protestants*, 16–24.

Bridge of Ten Thousand Ages on the Min River

Having become familiar with part of the island, Sophie felt confident to explore the area across the Bridge of Ten Thousand Ages. The bridge itself, bustled with people heading to and from the Old City, just over a couple of miles away. On her left, she passed the large YMCA building set up by the American Methodists and, on either side of the road, a scattering of rudimentary houses in which families lived outside the walled city. Continuing up the road, she reached one of seven turreted gates leading into Foochow. More than half a million people lived there in two-, three- or sometimes four-storey buildings, with shops below and living areas above. Main thoroughfares were paved with stones and often strung with colorful banners containing large Chinese characters. During busy periods, these streets were full of Chinese from every social level—field-women carrying heavy buckets suspended from a pole over their shoulders, men pulling rickshaws with a passenger, shopkeepers standing outside their premises, and artisans working with silver, brass, lacquer, and embroidery. Lepers and beggars loitered in some of the streets, and women with bound feet sat in doorways, surrounded by their half-naked children. Sophie began to see at first hand that in some respects China was "a sad, dark land" in need of Christian compassion and hope.

As she walked on, two imposing structures came into view, the ninth-century Black Pagoda and the even more striking tenth-century White Pagoda. Their original purpose had been to house relics and sacred writings and, like steeples attached to churches, a visual reminder of the importance of religious practices. There were several temples in the city, two of them near the pagodas, with a steady stream of people going in and out to perform their religious duties.

In April, after moving into the CMS Ladies' Home on the island, Sophie received some letters from home. The economic situation seemed to be gradually improving and, on the domestic front, news came of her sister Amy's wedding at St Luke's Burwood, with uncle William and Canon Moreton officiating.[10] Though pleased a relationship she had encouraged was now sealed in marriage, reading the letters made her realize how much she missed her family.

View over Nantai Island to the Old City of Foochow

Early May brought Sophie her first taste of a typical Chinese celebration. This was the Feast of the Dragon Boats, instituted in the memory of a venerable fourth-century BC statesman. On the Min, competing teams rowed dragon-shaped boats to the rhythm of pounding drums and the shouts of excited crowds. The following month, she took part in a special

---

10. Included was a lengthy, undated, clipping from *The Sydney Morning Herald* describing who was there, what the women wore, and details of the reception at her grandmother's Sydney residence.

A LITTLE BAND OF SISTERS IN "NO-MAN'S" LAND

Commonwealth celebration, Queen Victoria's Diamond Jubilee, organized by the British Consulate. In July, as the typhoon season was drawing near, everyone began to watch the skies carefully for any sign of the swirling tropical storms that could deluge the city, cause floods, and destroy property.

This was the prelude to the hot season that lasted until September. To avoid the debilitating heat, as well as regular outbreaks of malaria, typhoid and "summer diarrhoea" most Westerners, moved to Kuliang where the temperature was usually ten degrees cooler. This mountain retreat was two and a half thousand feet high, just eight miles from Foochow. It could be reached in four hours by sedan chair or a full day's walk. Surrounding hills were covered by pine trees and bamboos, and valleys were terraced with crops of rice and sweet potatoes. Dozens of stone houses were scattered around the main valley, as well as a post office, chapel, and tennis courts. There was an international clubhouse for social gatherings, lectures, plays, religious meetings, including CMS' annual Conference. A nearby village was provided essential goods, services, and workers during the summer months.

Sophie was keen to attend the Conference, partly because it was modeled on the Keswick Convention held in the Lake District around the same time. Like the majority of missionaries at that time, she was influenced by the spirituality of the evangelical, interdenominational movement that informed it.[11] She was also eager to meet the survivors of the Flower Mountain massacre, as well as those who had taken the place of its victims. During the build-up to the Conference, she was able to catch up with Amy Oxley and hear about her small dispensary in the village of Deng-doi, a day's travel by foot and sedan chair north-east of Foochow.

At the Conference itself, she learned that the current year had seen a twenty-five percent increase in missionaries coming to Fukien, mainly single women who now made up almost three-quarters of all serving there. As places of appointment for newcomers were announced at the Conference, she wondered where this would be? Since, outside foreign enclaves like the British Legation Church in Peking, the office of deaconess was not yet recognized by the church in China, there was no equivalent position in Fukien, or anywhere else in southern China. This meant that, even if work she took up entailed aspects of what a deaconess did, this would always be carried out incognito. Though willing to go to Kucheng where three of her

---

11. A classic early account of this phenomenon is by Pierson, *The Keswick Movement*. For its impact on mission in China, see the Appendix.

Australian predecessors had been killed, Sophie's only concern was serving people wherever that would be most helpful.

On completion of language study, she was delighted to hear that the Women's Sub-Committee had appointed her and Minna Searle, a recruit from Tasmania, to work with fellow-countrywoman Amy Oxley in the district of Lieng Kong. Its capital, Lieng Kong City, had a small church led by a Chinese pastor, an itinerant catechist, and a few bible women, but no resident missionaries. CMS had decided to start a mission station in Deng-doi, a large village not far from the district capital. It was unusual for such an initiative to be staffed only by women. At a time when colonials were often regarded by English authorities as inferior, choosing three Australian women to begin such a work was ground-breaking.[12]

In October, Sophie heard that Eliza Saunders, the widowed mother of the two sisters who were massacred at Kucheng, was arriving in Foochow. She had originally planned to come to Fukien with her daughters as a self-supported missionary, but the 1890s Depression had prevented her from selling the family home in Melbourne to fund this. Still holding true to her missionary commitment, five years later she was reaching Foochow to become house-keeper at the CMS Ladies House where Sophie was staying. The two of them regarded it as a "divine happenstance" that for a time they were living in the same place.

At the beginning of December, Sophie passed her first language exam, giving her a basic proficiency in reading and speaking the language. It was then time to apply for an internal passport from the British Consul to live and work outside of Foochow. This provided her with protection if local officials became difficult or exceeded their authority. Three days before Christmas, they traveled to Lieng Kong City where they were met by Amy, who was living there until their new home was completed in Deng-doi. On Christmas Day 1897 the three women visited the local church, where they were warmly received and assured of the prayers and support of the congregation. Finally, on New Year's Day 1898, they made a two hour journey to their new quarters.

梁劉柔芬

Their house was built on the side of a small hill overlooking the village and the Lieng river.

---

12. See further Frances Slater, *Wolfe Sisters of Foochow*, 61.

> Our new home is in a village of 2000 families some six miles from Lieng Kong city... Miss Searle, Miss Newton and I live together and very happy we are. Our nearest missionary neighbour (Mr Light in the next district) is thirty miles away and the missionary in charge of our District (Archdeacon Wolfe in the capital) is thirty miles away.[13]

Though in letters to others, the three women referred to each other formally, in private Sophie was called "Cissie," derived from "S.S.," her first two initials.

Deng-doi was a typical Fukienese village with a range of shops, several communal wells, and a number of small shrines and temples. Every five days there was a market that brought in farmers from the surrounding countryside. There was no local school, but itinerant scholars sometimes passed through, offering instruction to boys whose families were willing to pay for their services. There were also wandering blacksmiths who sold and made tools. Every so often there was a large-scale wedding or funeral, a performance in the village theatre, and a religious procession or observances. Although men occasionally visited other villages or the nearby provincial city, many women never went more than a few miles from home during their entire lives.[14]

The three women at Deng-doi worked very much as a team. While each had their own particular tasks, they also regularly assisted each other. They were assisted by a Chinese watchman, who looked after the property, especially when two of the women were away itinerating, and a cook, who bought, grew, and prepared food for their meals. Amy's dispensary was open all day twice a week, attracting dozens of sick people from the village and miles away. While queueing for help, a bible woman chatted with them and sought to share the gospel. Among those seeking medical attention were parents of blind children, and in time Amy felt compelled to start a small school for blind boys.[15] Minna and Sophie still had to spend several hours a day in language study. Apart from this, Minna assisted a

---

13. Amy Oxley, Letters from China, 27 February 1988. Amy described her life and work at Deng-doi in regular letters to her sister that are available in Welch, *Amy Oxley*, on which we drew heavily in our biography *They Shall See His Face*, 31–55.

14. Smith, *Village Life in China*, presents a varied and detailed account of life in Chinese villages at this time.

15. The full story of thie school, which later moved to the capital and became nationally as well as internationally well-known, is told in our biography of Amy Oxley, *They Shall See His Face*.

bible woman to undertake evangelism in a number of the closer villages. She also helped a catechist to prepare for Sunday services which were held in a temporary wooden building near their house.

Meanwhile Sophie, who was further along in language study, as well as helping out in the dispensary when needed, set up the first Day School for girls in the district. The curriculum included such basic subjects as reading, writing, and maths; hygiene and home management; biblical and religious instruction. As more bible-women were needed for the district, she began planning towards the establishment of a three-month long Women's Boarding School to train them.

During the first few months, the three missionaries were pleased to welcome groups of curious onlookers who were eager to see inside their new home, as well as observe the minute details of their daily lives. "It's a very good place to invite them into the Chinese Guest Room, and then play the organ, sing a hymn, and explain the meaning."[16] While this opened up contact with many in the village, living under the spotlight of so many prying eyes was not easy for them, even for more informal Australians![17]

---

16. Amy Oxley, Annual Letter, 29 November 1898, 1.

17. An excellent survey of the work undertaken by women missionaries in this period is provided by Welch, "Women's Work for Women." While girls and women were certainly the focus of their activities, they were involved in educating boys as well as girls, and men often eavesdropped when they were speaking.

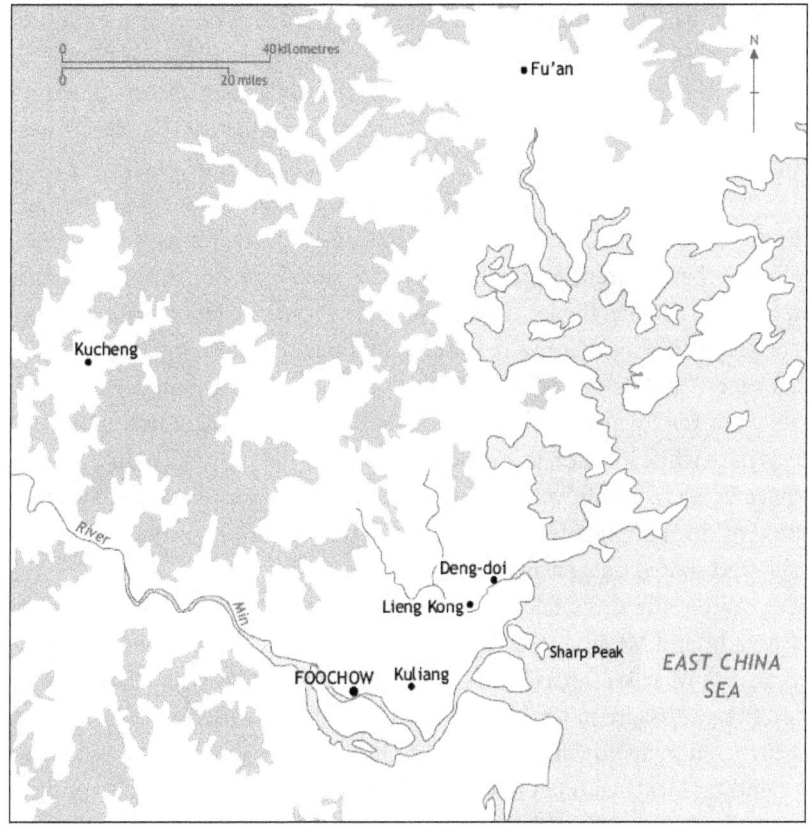

Places Sophie served during her years in China

In the wider district of Lieng Kong, an area of around forty square miles, travel was mainly along rough dirt tracks through fields or up and down hills. Villages near the sea concentrated on catching swordfish, prawns, and clams; those on the plain grew staples like rice and tea, but also sweet potatoes, beans, and watermelons. There were about two hundred villages and twelve towns in the district, some with quaint names like Long Dragon or Horse Snout.[18]

For the most part, Deng-doi had a moderate climate, tempered by its proximity to the sea. In the hot months, there was a danger of typhoons blowing in from the South China Sea. That summer, one tore the roof off their new house, flooded every room, and destroyed many of their

---

18. A good description of the district of Lieng Kong may be found in Stock, *For Christ and Fuh-kien*, 1904, 51–58.

possessions. The damage was so great that Minna had to return for a time to Foochow, and Amy decided to visit a number of villages, leaving only Sophie in Deng-doi. Fortunately, though this was when cholera or plague tended to spread among the densely-packed population, this year these were not a problem.

During the first few months at Deng-doi, issues of food and dress and food were a matter of discussion. For the most part, their meals were generally not that different from what they had eaten back home. With a largely temperate climate, the local district offered a great variety of fruit and vegetables. In spring there were oranges and bananas and, most of the year, cabbages, cauliflowers, carrots and potatoes. Milk and butter were available, but the former came from buffalo rather than cows, and the second was pure white in color, tasting like lard. Bread was only baked in the cities. Since Western goods were expensive, many missionaries asked for them to be sent from home. Sweets or "lollies" were often received with child-like glee and shared out sparingly with housemates.

While the three fellow-workers would have preferred to follow the China Inland Mission [CIM] practice of wearing Chinese dress, they continued to wear Western clothes. Though, initially, it was also CMA policy, after the massacre in Kucheng CMS missionaries working in Fukien were instructed to avoid Chinese attire. Doing this, it was argued, would avoid offending locals who felt that missionaries were inappropriately trying to pass themselves off as Chinese.

As the year progressed, Sophie began to experience severe headaches. While itinerating in a nearby village, Amy wrote that "Poor Cissie's head is so bad that she is still to have perfect rest in Ning-Tak [hospital]. It is such a disappointment to us all and will mean extra work for me and Minna."[19] At first, these migraines were regarded as a consequence of her stressful ongoing language study. However, as the months passed, they recurred and were probably linked to her monthly cycle. They often wiped her out of action for days at a stretch, requiring complete bed rest in a quiet, dark room. On these occasions, Sophie felt useless, especially when her colleagues had to care for her. Despite pleading with God to take this affliction away, like Paul's "thorn in the flesh," it eventually became a means for God to remind her that "my grace is sufficient for you, for my power is made perfect in weakness" (2 Cor. 12:7).

---

19. Amy Oxley: Letters from China, 27 February 1898.

The women's vision for the work in Deng-doi involved three major building projects—the women's boarding school, a permanent church building, and a small hospital. In April 1898, Sophie heard that the money for the first project, her womens school, had come through. Immediately they began looking for a suitable block of land nearby. Shortly afterward, the good news came that she had passed the second Chinese exam, recognizing her basic fluency.[20] What for most missionaries took two years to achieve, Sophie had accomplished in just fifteen months. The additional Chinese name students now gave her was "Auntie Teacher."

As the three women developed closer links with some of the villagers, they began to receive invitations to special celebrations such as weddings.

> The house we went to is not very grand. Just inside the front door there is a room with an earth floor and various tubs, fishing nets, etc, all about. The next room is like it but today had two square tables spread ready for the feast, that is, there were about eight saucers full of things. We were invited to sit down and the bride was brought out of the bedroom for us to look at. Poor thing, she was not allowed to speak and she did look miserable, her hair was covered with ornaments and she had on a red dress. After standing for us to gaze at, she was turned to face the wall and left standing in that position. The eating soon began and it was not really bad. We were not pressed to eat, the bride sat at the other (inferior) table and was not given anything. After about an hour and a half it was over. I was glad because it is tiring sitting so long not talking, and having four dirty hungry dogs under the table all the time is not pleasant. We came to this feast because they are all Christians except the bride, three members were baptised lately. We were invited into the bride's bedroom and then, contrary to custom, talked. The bride had a sore foot and asked for medicine and so I sent up for some at once.[21]

This was not the only way in which the women became involved in the lives of villagers. Occasionally they were called to intervene in a serious dispute between men that threatened to become violent, or became involved in questioning the wisdom of betrothing of a younger girl to an older male who already had several wives.

---

20. This took place on May 11, 1898, and is referred to in the margin of her Prayer Book at the appropriate point in the church year.

21. Amy Oxley, Letters from China, 7 and 11 May 1898.

Along with developing closer relationships with people in the villages, the three colleagues looked forward to letters from home which could take up to six weeks to arrive. A mailboat came up fortnightly from Foochow, and letters from family and supporters, sometimes with newspaper clippings, were eagerly read and reread in the days that followed. Sophie was a conscientious correspondent, and usually had written a batch of letters to send in the next post. Towards the end of the year, news came that her younger brother Herbert had married his fiancée, Olive.

Reliable transport was a constant problem for the mission. Chinese porters would sometimes promise to carry them and their luggage for a fixed sum, then refuse to do so or charge them more when some were under the influence of opium or it looked like bad weather. With a large unexpected gift, Amy decided to purchase a boat, aptly called the *Messenger of Peace*. This made trips to Foochow easier and shorter than going by foot over mountainous terrain. It also enabled the women to make visits to villages along the river or coast more quickly and regularly.[22] Although there was the possibility of being held up by robbers, this was just as often a threat when traveling overland.

Another recurrent problem was workmen failing to turn up because something more appealing had come their way. So, the women asked the mission's handyman decided to learn some basic carpentry and building skills and were then able to help him add a visitor's room to their residence for occasional guests. Along with a few local Christians, they renovated and extended a nearby vacant house for use as a church on Sundays and other meetings during the week.

The women were greatly encouraged by the fact that more men were eavesdropping on their Bible talks held in women's homes. Despite it being generally unacceptable in Chinese culture for women to teach men, sometimes up to twenty gathered outside to listen. Through one of these meetings, a practitioner of Chinese medicine, and as a fortune-teller, were converted, the latter publicly chopping in half the idol he had used to divine the future. Another convert was a well-known "Vegetarian" in the village. This inevitably reminded the women of the Kucheng incident which had spurred their decision to come to China. In all this, as Sophie

---

22. "A Little Colony in Southern China," *Bowral Free Press*, 10 May. 1900, 4 in which Amy is described by Minna Searle as a "master mariner."

noted, it was through patient, untiring dedication that people were drawn "one by one" to Christ.²³

梁劉柔芬

Faraway Pagoda in Lieng Kong District

23. S. Newton, Annual Letter, November 1898, 2.

In early 1899, with Minna also having completed her language study, the three women were free to extend their work into unreached parts of the Lieng Kong district. To do this properly, they decided to go to a place which would give them a birds-eye view of the region. On a steep hill south of their mission station sat an ancient pagoda. They decided this would make a good vantage point. One morning, they set out on the two-hour walk across the plain. On reaching the summit they found a small temple served by a few Buddhist monks. In several places, the pagoda itself was crumbling from centuries of exposure to the weather. From its highest level, there opened up

> a splendid view of the plain. We counted nearly a dozen villages within quite an easy walking distance on this side of the river, numbers more on the other side, and away six miles up the river could be seen the crowded city of Lieng Kong. Again, as we turned in the direction of Foochow, we saw other villages dotted here and there along the coast, and others sheltering away in little bays. We could hardly get a more extensive view as we stood on that old and broken-down pagoda. Such a view makes us feel 'What are we among so many? Thank God it is not by power, but by His Spirit, souls are won'.[24]

As the women talked on, they recalled the vision God gave Abraham of the new land spread out before him, in which his children would multiply. Just as he had to believe this against all odds, so this little band of sisters had to trust God for the work he had called them to do. As well as continuing the work in Deng-doi, Sophie would begin to focus more on developing it in the city of Lieng Kong. Amy, with the help of a catechist, would concentrate on settlements upriver from Deng-doi and down the coast. Minna, would give more attention to the remaining villages, four of which had a catechist.

In the following months, however, Sophie's migraines flared up again. The pain and resulting exhaustion were so bad that she was admitted to Tak-Dai Hospital in Foochow for several weeks to fully recover. Upon her return, she could only cope with part-time responsibilities, and was frustrated by the extra burden this placed on her colleagues.

By the summer of 1899, several more families in Deng-doi had given up their household gods and more individuals were coming forward for baptism and confirmation. The little church in the village, under the

---

24. S. Newton, Annual Letter, 22 November 1899.

leadership of a Chinese catechist, was becoming more united and increasing in size. One of the strengths of CMS in the Fukien Province, despite its hierarchical Anglican character, was its more egalitarian approach to the Chinese Christians. It was strongly committed to the principles of self-propagation, self-government, and self-support for the local church, with missionaries playing a supportive and training role. In all these respects, Sophie, Amy, and Minna saw themselves primarily as partners and enablers of indigenous church life.

In early October, the Women's School at Deng-doi finally opened, with sixteen students enrolled, most of whom were recent converts. Sometimes their husbands were agreeable to this arrangement because they had two or more wives, and for a short period did not have to support one of them. At other times, they wanted their wives to stay at home and look after them, only giving their consent after much persuasion by one of the missionaries. The latter arrangement was usually a fragile one, with jealous and dominating husbands frequently recalling their wives halfway through their course. The season long curriculum involved such topics as the Ten Commandments, Lord's Prayer, Apostle's Creed, and the so-called "Hundred Texts", basic biblical passages that summed up the heart of the Christian message.[25] Students were also taught to read and write in anglicized Chinese and, on completion of the course, became evangelists and suppliers of literature among their neighbors and in nearby villages.[26]

Meanwhile, her work in the Girls School continued to develop. A big help was acquiring some Christian classics that had been translated into Chinese, such as John Bunyan's *The Pilgrim's Progress*, as well as monthly Christian children's magazines. She was also grateful for the contribution of materials and literature for the students from Sower's Bands, mostly made up of young supporters of the CMA in Australia.

Through both the Girls and Womens Schools, Sophie encouraged students to look beyond traditional female roles that were so common in China, especially in rural areas. These were well described in a popular Chinese poem:

> How sad it is to be a woman!
> Nothing on earth is held so cheap.

---

25. These were originally compiled by Protestants to counter Catholic claims in Ireland, and a commentary was written by Hammond, *The Hundred Texts*, who later became Principal of Moore Theological College, Sydney.

26. Amy Oxley, Letters to China, 18 April 1899.

> Boys stand leaning at the door
> Like Gods fallen out of Heaven.
> Their hearts brave the Four Oceans,
> The wind and dust of a thousand miles.
> No one is glad when a girl is born:
> By her the family sets no store.
> Then she grows up, she hides in her room
> Afraid to look a man in the face.
> No one cries when she leaves her home—
> Sudden as clouds when the rain storms
> She bows her head and composes her face,
> Her teeth are pressed on her red lips:
> She bows and kneels countless times.
> She must humble herself even to the servants.
> His love is distant as the stars in Heaven,
> Yet the sunflower bends toward the sun.
> Their hearts more sundered than water and fire—
> A hundred evils are heaped upon her.
> Her face will follow the years' changes:
> Her lord will find new pleasures.
> They that were once like substance and shadow . . .[27]

It was this attitude that led men to regard education for females as a waste of money and time. They also saw it as a hindrance to proposals of marriage for their daughters that would bring a good price. In its place, Sophie and her colleagues sought to give girls and women a greater vision of who they could become and what they could do, both inside and outside the home.

---

27. The poem dates back to Fu Xuan in. the third century BCE but remained popular down through the centuries,

A LITTLE BAND OF SISTERS IN "NO-MAN'S" LAND

Sophie and the Girls School choir in Deng-doi

In late December 1899, the mission station at Deng-doi was woken by the sound of Christmas carols being sung by students from Amy's Blind Boys School. Although some villagers reacted negatively to the celebration of this Western festival, and there was even the threat of violence, nothing more came of this. However, over the last few months the women had been receiving reports of growing militancy against foreigners in other parts of China. Many of the hostilities involved a group described as the Boxer Movement. It was not a good note on which to start the new century.

3

Chinese Whispers and Witness in the Fading Middle Kingdom

WITH SCHOOLS CLOSED DOWN from the end of January for two weeks during Chinese New Year, Sophie looked forward to taking a break at "The Firs" in Foochow. Celebrations in the capital, heralding the "Year of the Rat," were more colorful than anything she had experienced in Dengdoi or the city of Lieng Kong. It was a highpoint of the year—a time for gathering for family banquets, offering hospitality and exchanging gifts, visiting temples to gain good fortune from the gods, settling accounts, and repaying or reclaiming debts.

Shops were impressively decorated with banners, golden flowers, and red gilt-edged paper adorned with blessings. Outside family homes, fireworks were set off to protect their inhabitants from evil spirits. Clashing gongs, shrieking flutes, twirling swordsmen, acrobatic jugglers, and entertaining actors filled the streets. The half-mile-long Dragon Procession was surrounded by cannonades of firecrackers that drew gasps of amazement from adults and children alike. These events culminated in the spectacle of the Lantern Festival, with many yellow lights of all shapes and sizes rising to the heavens.

This holiday provided most missionaries with an opportunity to visit friends, share in the celebrations, and catch up on some personal errands. Visiting shops and businesses before or after the holiday gave opportunity, as one lady missionary wrote, for arranging to see "the tailor, curio vender, dentist and, probably the photographer . . . shopping and sending parcels back home . . . quite a little whirl of excitement."[1]

On returning to Deng-doi, Sophie was delighted that enrolments at the Women's School had risen to twenty six. Since this exceeded the number that could fit the building, extra space had to be commandeered in the church. A Matron also had to be found to help look after the women. Larger numbers of children were also attending her Sunday School classes and over forty were coming to the Wednesday choir practice. More than sixty patients were being treated weekly at the Dispensary, with the names of nearly twelve hundred on its medical register. Though a thief had recently broken into Amy's Blind School it and stolen a few clothes, it was full with fifteen boys. In order to have greater access to outlying parts of the district, Minna had set up permanent headquarters in another village. All in all, the women felt, "God is working a most wonderful way here just now."[2]

Minna, Sophie and Amy with a Women's School class

At this time, Sophie experienced a significant new development in her personal life.

The background to this took place in Foochow, when one of the local literati working for the Qing dynasty unexpectedly failed an important imperial examination. This was his worst nightmare and became so desperate that

1. Darley, *Light of the Morning*, 126.
2. Amy Oxley, Letters from China, 19 March 1900.

he lost his sanity, became an opium addict, and frequently abused his wife and two children. Totally disillusioned, his wife, Ding Ngu Sëük-ching, ran away from home with the two children, one a 7-year-old boy named Ding Daik-hok, the other an infant girl named Ding Ai-cio. They were reduced to living and begging in the streets, where one day a Christian giving money mentioned that there were missionaries in the adjacent district of Liengkong who could offer them shelter. This encouraged the mother to walk for several days, in some pain, with the children to Deng-doi. When they arrived at the mission, it was Sophie, who gave the three a very warm reception and arranged accommodation for them. From the beginning, she took a close interest in their welfare, regarding them as if they were her relatives. Sophie encouraged the mother to take part in the Women's School and, when she had finished the training, supported her as a bible-woman working alongside her or a colleague in the local village.

The month of May marked an important milestone for CMS in China as fifty years earlier, the first missionary had arrived in Foochow. Sophie and her colleagues had been working towards the Jubilee celebrations with great anticipation for many months and looking forward to Bishop Hoare's visit. As he was based in Hong Kong, and could only occasionally come to Fukien, let alone to a village rather than city, this was a special occasion. On 8 May,

> everyone was excited and on the lookout as the Christians wished to go and welcome him. I was over at the school giving the 23 women who were to be confirmed final reminders of what they were to do and say ... A messenger came to tell us the glad news, the Bishop has come, so then I went over to our house and we had afternoon tea and discussed plans etc. Then the Bishop went over to the Women's House and spoke very nicely.

Women missionaries' house at Deng-doi

At 7.30pm after visiting the Bible Women's House, we had the Confirmation Service. It was beautiful. I do wish you had been there to see first the men and the 23 women, one by one go up to the rails and kneel there, receiving we believe a blessing from God Himself . . . After the service we sang 'O Jesus I have promised to serve thee to the end'.

The next morning we partook, over 70 altogether of the Lord's Supper . . . we need to pray very definitely for the native Christians. Some women will be soon returning to their villages and will not perhaps have the opportunity at again partaking for months or years. May their love and desire to serve Him not grow cold . . . The Bishop gave a very helpful Bible reading on 2 Corinthians 5. The part that came to the three of us was that we are ambassadors for Christ, and that we have to plead with these people, beseech them, and pray for them . . . not just to deliver the message.

About 3.30pm the next day the Bishop and Mr Lloyd [were leaving] for Foochow . . . outside our house were standing a number of Christian men and the catechist who let off crackers . . . which drew an extra 30 day school children and about 60 women . . . it was such a nice sight.

I would like those who disbelieve in missionary work to visit this school. We thank God for several girls in this District who were trained there and are now married and teachers of our village day schools. One is the teacher in Miss Newton's Women's School.³

梁劉柔芬

From the beginning of the year, stories about occasional animosity towards foreigners, including missionaries, in northern China began to spread. This was a reminder that in some places attitudes that lay behind the massacre in Kucheng five years earlier continued to surface. The unjust treaties imposed on China by European nations after the Opium Wars in the 1840s and 1860s had not been forgotten, and there was growing resentment over the intrusion of foreign-owned telegraphs, railways, and mission stations into the countryside. Meanwhile, the opium trade continued to addict growing numbers of men, and destroy whole families. Viewing Japan's rise as a consequence of its adopting some Western innovations, in the 1890s the Qing Dynasty decided to follow suit. The increasing unrest resulting from all these factors strengthened the appeal of secret societies such as the I Ho Ch'uan, or the "Righteous and Harmonious Fists." These so-called "Boxers" were initially convinced that their religious ceremonies and martial arts made them invincible in battle, though later they began to rely on Western weaponry. Their basic goal was to overthrow the Qing dynasty, destroy railways, mines, and churches, and to execute or at least expel all foreigners.

Their aggressive attitude had:

> ... many interesting parallels to events in the early 21st century. It saw an uprising in a non-Western country against what was seen as the corrupting influence of Western practices and ideologies. In some respects, it was a foretaste of the current war against terrorism, in that a basically grass roots movement fought what they saw as a holy war against a technologically superior collection of foreign powers to preserve their values and beliefs.⁴

Their struggle was primarily anti-Western and only secondarily anti-Christian. It was not so much that the missionaries' religious beliefs were offensive, but rather the way their converts were perceived to be flouting traditional ceremonies and family obligations.⁵ As the year progressed,

---

3. Amy Oxley. Letters from China, 16 May 1900.

4. See further Dugdale-Pointon, TDP. 19 September 2004, *The Boxer Rebellion, 1900,* at http://www.historyofwar.org/articles/wars.boxer.html.

5. An early account of this movement was provided by Edwards, *Fire and Sword in*

missionaries became prime targets in remote areas where official protection was weak and the general populace more superstitious. In these regions, the presence of Christianity was blamed for the famine that had resulted from a disastrous spring and summer, the driest on record.

Boxer soldiers armed for battle

In late May 1900, news about the Boxer uprising became more disturbing. Following a riot in a village near Peking, two British missionaries were killed. By June, harassment and attacks on foreigners and missionaries increased. In another northern village, sixty Chinese Catholic men, women, and children were slaughtered. In the following weeks, stories emerged of mobs surrounding mission stations and dragging out their occupants, killing some on the spot and taking others to temples to be tortured. Thousands of Chinese converts were hacked to pieces, set alight or skinned alive.

Shan-si. 58–59, and a fully researched later one by Diana Preston, *The Boxer Rebellion.*

A well-known Boxer hymn that had appeared widely in the Chinese press set out explicitly the main aims and goals of the uprising.

> The gods assist the Boxers,
> The patriotric harmonious corps.
> It is because the foreign devils disturb the Middle Kingdom,
> Urging their people to join their religion,
> To turn their backs to Heaven,
> Venerate not the gods and abandon their ancestors . . .
> Foreign devils are not produced by mankind,
> If you doubt this,
> Look at them carefully,
> The eyes of foreign devils are bluish.
> No rain falls,
> The earth is getting dry,
> That is because the Christian religion stops the heavens.
> The gods are angry,
> The genii are vexed . . .
> Burn up the yellow written prayers,
> Light up the incense sticks,
> To invite the gods and genii of all the grottos.
> The gods will come down from the mountains,
> And support the human bodies to practice the Hp Ch'uan.
> When all the military accomplishments or tactics
> Are fully learned,
> It will not be difficult to exterminate the foreign devils then,
> Push aside the railway track,
> Pull out the telegraph poles:
> Immediately after this destroy the steamers . . .
> Let the foreign devils all be killed,
> May the whole elegant Empire
> Of the great China dynasty be ever prosperous.[6]

On 21 June, the Dowager Empress issued a proclamation that concluded:

---

6. "Two Proclamations of the Boxers" at https://college.cengage.com › primary sources › world

> Foreign religions are reckless and oppressive, disrespectful to the gods and oppressive to the people. The Righteous People will burn and kill. Your judgments from Heaven are about to come. Turn from the heterodox and revert to the true. Is it not benevolence to exhort you people of the Christian Religion? . . . If you do your duty, you are good people. If you do not repent there will be no opportunity for after-regret. For this purpose is this proclamation put forth. Let all comply with it.[7]

A third of a million Boxers, with support from elements in the Chinese Army, besieged more than a thousand Westerners—including missionaries and their families, and three thousand Chinese Christians—in the foreign legations in Peking. Newspapers carried daily reports of these developments, sometimes under horrific headlines that sometimes exaggerated or falsified what was happening. These accounts became headline stories around the world, and the Australian missionaries' families and friends, including Sophie's, were deeply concerned and fearful for their safety.

Fortunately, there were no obvious signs of Boxer sympathizers in Lieng Kong, nor of any militancy among supporters of the loosely connected "Vegetarian" movement. But further unsettling news from northern China persuaded the Chinese Viceroy and British Consul to order all missionaries into Foochow for protection. For other reasons, the three women had earlier decided to spend the hot summer period outside their district. Sophie and Minna had decided to visit Japan and learn more about mission work there: Amy was due to return to Australia for a year on her first furlough. Then, on 1 July, there was a further proclamation from the Qing Government in Peking ordering the expulsion of all foreigners from China and the persecution of local Christians. However, the more moderate Viceroy in Foochow decided to ignore this edict.

News now reached Foochow that, in parts of the province, sympathizers with the Boxers had plundered property, beaten a number of people, and killed one person. A few days later, there were reports of antagonism against Westerners in Foochow itself. To their relief, the ship on which Sophie and Minna had booked a passage was ready to sail to Yokahama. Shortly after it left, intelligence indicated that protesters were planning a march to Nantai Island where most foreigners, including missionaries, lived. There were fears that this could boil over into looting, lighting of fires, and destruction of buildings. The very day the trouble was expected

---

7. Drawn from Hnhyedu.net. April 23 2011.

to happen, the rising waters of the Min after heavy summer rains flooded nearby parts of the city, made it impossible to get to Nantai. "Though this was a terrible disaster," wrote Eugene Stock, "[it] seems in God's providence to have been a powerful deterrent to those who plotted evil."[8]

In mid-July, a magazine appeared in Australia, featuring a story on "Imperilled Australian Missionaries in China," with photographs of Sophie, Amy, Minna, and sixteen others.[9] Articles like these led to an official enquiry by the Australian Government about the status of its missionaries in Fukien, and its subsequent decision to send a small force to Peking. On 23 July, however, the British Consul in Foochow was able to guarantee the protection of all missionaries in the province. He confirmed that the capital was quiet and the missionaries safe. In early August, a twenty-thousand strong international force finally reached the besieged foreign legations in Peking and by 14 August the danger was over. During the Boxer Rebellion, it was estimated more than two hundred and forty missionaries were killed, three-quarters of whom were Protestant, as well as around eight thousand Chinese Christians, the majority of them Catholics.[10]

8. Stock, *For Christ and Fuh-kien*, 37.

9. Stead, "Imperilled Missionaries in China."

10. As Broomhall, *Martyred Missionaries,* documents, the majority of the Protestant missionaries worked with the CIM.

Photos taken at the height of the Boxer Rebellion

Since occasional conflict with the Boxers continued in northern and inland China, Sophie and Minna had to remain in Japan for a further two months. It was not until November that they received permission from the British Consul in Foochow to return to the province. After spending time in Yokohama and Tokyo, Sophie wrote: "we had an opportunity of seeing something of the wonderful methods of working in that little kingdom, so interesting and beautiful, so wonderfully open to Western education but content without the Gospel [in the CMS missions,] it was a privilege indeed to see God's work in the hearts of many, and several of the native workers with whom I came into contact were as bright and earnest as Christians at home. I enjoyed my visit very much indeed but was delighted to return to the land of my adoption." So far as her work was concerned, "It is a trial to us not to be able to return to our stations, but we feel the testing will be good for our dear Christians, and this will doubtless show us more clearly those who are true."[11]

Finally, in February 1901, after eight months away, Sophie and Minna received their internal passports from the British Consul, and within a few days traveled back to Deng-doi. To their delight, wrote Minna, "the Christians came up to greet us on our arrival and gave us a very hearty welcome."[12] After settling back into their home, the two women looked forward to a week's trip around the closest villages. This was the prelude to a longer visit to fourteen villages in the district where there were small groups of Christians. On their return, Sophie wrote: "We were thankful to find how many had stood firm, but still we did see some who had grown cold, and others who do not walk with us now."[13]

While these activities seemed to rejoin the threads broken by the Uprising, this was only temporary. The team of three was now in the midst of change. Amy was only staying briefly at Deng-doi before transferring her Blind School to a permanent location in Foochow, and being replaced by Nellie Marshall, a registered nurse from Sydney. Minna was working in another village that gave her better access to more distant settlements. Meanwhile, general supervision of the work in Lieng Kong was handed over to the Rev John Martin, Principal of the Theological College, with whom Sophie had first stayed in Foochow. As, on Amy Oxley's upcoming furlough, Sophie was shortly to become Senior Missionary in the district, this was a welcome development.

梁劉柔芬

She soon began to recruit students for the re-opening of the Women's School, and by early spring the Girls School was also under way. A great asset to evangelistic work in the village was the gift of a magic lantern and

11. S. S. Newton, *CMS Gleaner*, 5 December 1900, 664–65.
12. M. Searle. Annual Letter, 11 February 1901.
13. S. S. Newton, Annual Letter, 20 November 1901.

slides. This enabled the catechist to put on shows for a wide-eyed audience of adults and children. Many women who attended said that they could now see, as well as hear, the Bible brought to life, and increasing numbers of men were also intrigued to watch screenings from the sidelines.

By the end of the school year, each of the women felt that their nerves had been frayed by the long hours and multiple demands of their work. An added danger was becoming so preoccupied with it that there was no room for any other personal or wider interest. The excessive heat and humidity of summer tended to further deplete their remaining emotional reserves. Privately the women talked about becoming less patient and irritated in their day-to-day tasks, even in their relationships with one another. For her part, Sophie had developed certain habits that mostly helped guard against this. These included her love of gardening and knitting, going on long breaks in the summer, maintaining an interest in the people of Israel, taking days off to "wait on God"—and during busy furloughs, seeking a place for a few weeks where she could be completely on her own.

Just as the missionaries were beginning to feel more rested, cholera struck parts of the province. While their district was less affected than Foochow, where thousands fell sick and many died, they were fully stretched by the number of people seeking help. It was a cruel and frightening way for someone to die. For most, death came in a matter of days. The volume of patients indicated how much more than just a small infirmary was needed, especially since many villagers found it intimidating to go to a hospital in the city.

As her furlough drew near, Sophie wrote:

> Although it is nearly five years since I reached China, I feel as if I have only just begun my work, having suffered a good deal with my head: it has often kept me from doing what I wished and otherwise felt able to do, but I look forward to a furlough as a time in which to recruit for China, with the longing to come back and be able to work more faithfully for the Master among these dear people.[14]

Six weeks later, in the middle of February 1902, she boarded a ship to Hong Kong and, at the end of the month, set sail on the *SS Guthrie* for the three-week trip to Sydney. The country she returned to was different from the one she had left six years earlier. It was no longer a collection of individual colonies governing their own affairs, but now the Commonwealth

14. S. S. Newton, Annual Letter, 11 November and 2 December 1902, 2.

of Australia with its own home-grown Prime Minister.[15] One of the new Parliament's major decisions was sending sixteen thousand troops to South Africa to support Britain in the Boer War. That year, the Franchise Act gave Australian women the same rights to vote as men, only the second country in the world to do this.

The CMA NSW recorded how Sophie, and another returning missionary, were "stirring up our hearts by telling of what God had done through them."[16] Her priority was enjoying time with her mother and closer members of the family. Two of her younger sisters and brother were married and had children while she was away. She was eager to connect with her home church of St Paul's, Burwood, which had faithfully supported her work in Lieng Kong. CMA arranged deputation visits to adult and children's organizations, link churches, and several large interdenominational meetings in both city and country areas. Her addresses sought to raise awareness about the needs of China, and challenge hearers to pray for as well as consider missionary service.

During this furlough, Sophie was reminded of prejudices and misconceptions that many Australians, including Christians, held about the Chinese. While some of these were inflamed by the recent Immigration Restriction Act (or White Australia Policy) of 1901, antagonism stemmed from rivalry on the 1850s goldfields, labor shortages during the 1890s Depression, and sometimes just blind racism based on appearance and color. Since most Australians had not traveled outside their country, and most had little to do with local Chinese, negative attitudes were frequently based on rumors and one-eyed reporting.[17] In contrast to prevailing opinions, Sophie was pleased to see at first-hand the Anglican mission at Botany under the leadership of Rev George Soo Hoo Ten, which reached out to Chinese who frequented opium dens in the inner city and worked in market gardens on its southern edge.[18]

---

15. The earliest treatment of this came from Wise, *Making of the Australian Commonwealth*.

16. "Instructions to Miss S. S. Newton, Church Missionary Association," 21 September 1903.

17. Written a little later was Willard, *White Australia Policy* and, focusing on Chinese experience, Fitzgerald, *Big White Lie*.

18. See Ten, George Soo (1848–1934), *Australian Dictionary of Biography*, vol. 6, 1976 at the National Centre of Biography, Australian National University, https://adb.anu.edu.au/biography/ten-george-soo-hoo-4699/text778.

Chinese had been coming out to Australia since the gold rushes of the 1850s. Ninety-five percent were men arriving in groups from particular villages or districts, who sent back money regularly to families and went back to their homeland every few years. Once the lure of quick riches had dried up, many moved to the fringes of cities and country towns where they took up growing vegetables for sale or sometimes shop-keeping. By the turn of the century, there were an estimated twenty thousand Chinese in New South Wales alone, many of them from poorer districts around Foochow and Amoy in Fukien Province. Some of these had resided in Australia for two generations, raising families and contributing to the wider society, when shortly after Federation in the early 1900s the so-called White Australia Policy was introduced. This legislation not only put an end to further Chinese emigration, but expelled many who did not want to leave. This revealed a dark underside of racial intolerance in the nation and, despite increasing discomfort with it from the middle of the century, was not repealed until the mid-1970s.

梁劉柔芬

In September 1903, after eighteen months on furlough, Sophie prepared to leave Sydney on the SS *Empire* for Hong Kong and then Foochow. Arriving a month later, she found that during her time away postal and telegraph networks, as well as sea and rail systems, had further expanded throughout China. As yet, these had not noticeably affected Lieng Kong. Once she had received her internal passport from the British Consul, Sophie went on to Deng-doi.

Sadly, during her furlough, some converts in the village had given up their faith. This was partly because the church had been without a local catechist to lead it and often looked rather empty. However, she was encouraged by a relief missionary teacher's assessment of the village that "the best Christian women here are those who have been taught by Miss Newton."[19] As the year progressed, interest in both the Sunday service and the Saturday prayer meeting increased. This was helped by the coming of a new pastor in Lieng Kong city, who not only reinvigorated the church there but catechists in villages around the district. For Sophie, his arrival from

---

19. This was from E. Goldie, Annual Letter, 3 December 1902, 1, the sister-in-law of Rev John Martin, who Sophie had got to know during her first year in Foochow.

Kucheng, where the Stewarts and Saunders sisters were massacred ten years earlier, was tangible evidence of God's providence at work.

Her main desire was to see how Seuk-ching, Daik-hok, and Ai-cio were faring. Though she had kept in touch with them by letter during her furlough, she was eager to see them face-to-face. The first task was to organize repair of the Womens School, which had been damaged by a typhoon, recruit new students, and get it under way again. Resuming this work was "a very happy one."[20] While numbers initially were small, increasing interest in the surrounding villages soon led to the school having full enrolments. In watching the progress some of these women made, Sophie envisioned a day when the work bible-women did was recognized as similar to the ministry of deaconesses like herself. Her second responsibility was the Girls' Boarding School. As a result of deputations during the furlough, a few women in Australia offered to support individual students from poorer homes.

On the medical front, under Nellie Marshall's capable supervision, numbers at the dispensary gradually increased, with over a hundred patients coming each week. This growth led to more evangelistic opportunities. The following year, eight women and eleven children prepared for baptism, and between twenty and thirty for confirmation, among whom were the mission station's watchman and handyman-porter.[21] It was also encouraging to see the quality of those who had been converts for some time. The women agreed with the assessment of Bishop Hoare that;

> They know nothing of the many controversies which have rent the Church of Christ in times gone by. They know nothing of Calvinism or Arminianism, but yet they will without hesitation ascribe the fact that they are members of Christ to the Grace and Calling of God. They know nothing of the controversy about justification by faith, but yet they do know that they are sinners, that Christ has died to make atonement for their sins, and that by Him everyone that believeth is justified. And they have a very real belief in the power of the Holy Spirit to help them in the temptations and trials of their lives. And as to those lives, what shall I say? Not infrequently we have to lament over their falls, but more frequently are we permitted to rejoice over their victories.[22]

---

20. S. S. Newton, Annual Letter, 13 November 1904, 1.
21. Annual Report, Church Missionary Association NSW, 1904.
22. Recorded in Stock, *Church Missionary Society*, 314.

Unfortunately, it was during 1904 that but Seuk-ching fell seriously ill. Since the estranged father had died several years earlier, she pleaded with Sophie to look after Daik-hok and Ai-cio if the worst happened so they would not become orphans. After a short time, she did die and was buried in Dëng-döi. Sophie immediately arranged to become the children's guardian and from then on treated them as if they were her own. They quickly responded, and soon began calling her "Mother." As Daik-hok was an extremely smart boy, he was soon able to enter Trinity College on Nantai island and with the help of a bible-woman when she was itinerating, Sophie continued to care for young Ai-cio.

For most of the following year, Sophie was the only missionary at Deng-doi. Minna fell seriously ill and was ordered to take a medical furlough in Australia. Work in the villages suffered most from Minna's absence but, when opportunity arose, Sophie found that:

> One of the most encouraging features in this work is to be able to gather (within a very short period of time after our arrival) a little group of Christians (chiefly women) for a prayer meeting, varying in numbers from six to 12 in at least 10 different centres in the district. It does one good to hear the simple, heartfelt, earnest prayers, showing they know something of prayer, and they generally tell us some answer to prayer that they have had since our last visit. By staying a night, we can always get a nice congregation, when of course the men join in, and they greatly enjoy the singing.[23]

Understaffing also slowed up extending the ministry beyond poorer to wealthier women in Lieng Kong city. Doing this meant having the courage to wander in higher class neighborhoods in the hope of being invited into one of their "well-to-do" houses.[24] With so many new opportunities opening up, Sophie longed for more women, and men, to join them in the growing work.

Overall, however, the city

> seems to be wholly given up to idolatry . . . It is not nearly, as in some cases, purely for pleasure that they worship, but that here they really believe that the spirits can protect them. Consequently, just now [the city elders] are spending an enormous sum of money, extorted from the people, on a huge and hideous idol procession.[25]

---

23. S. S. Newton, Annual Letter, 10 November 1906, 1.

24. S. S. Newton, Annual Letter, 19 November 1906, 1–2.

25. S. S. Newton, Annual Letter, 27 November 1905, 1, which, interestingly, was

There, as in Deng-doi and other larger villages, opium dens also tempted men to imbibe, addicting them to the drug and depleting them of money their families desperately needed for food and clothing. Because of the shame involved, it was often difficult for their wives to appeal for help in dealing with addicted husbands. Knowing that most of the opium was a result of trading by English ships and companies only added to her frustration. In tackling issues of idolatry and addiction she wrote, echoing the apostle Paul, that though "we are hard pressed on every side, we are not crushed" (2 Corinthians 4:8).[26]

In early 1906, news came that both a Protestant and a Catholic mission had been burned down in the interior of Fukien Province. While the Chinese Viceroy again considered withdrawing all missionaries into the capital, his orders to execute the ringleader, and punish remaining offenders, were so quickly carried out that there was no need to act further. This incident was a reminder that, six years after the Boxer Uprising, threats to missionaries lay just below the surface.

When summer came, for the first time in two years the women in Deng-doi could all enjoy a lengthy break at Kuliang. From one simple villa twenty years earlier, this settlement had grown to over a hundred houses where many foreigners took their annual holiday, including some from other provinces. Along with "CMS Cottage," and related places such as "The Olives" and "The Bamboos," a map from the time shows one that was named "Australia House." For a small donation each year, residents could become members of the Kuliang Union, which organized public lectures and sacred concerts in the church.

---

written from the city of Lieng Kong itself rather than from Deng-doi.
26. S. S. Newton, Annual Letter, .27 November 1905, 1.

View over Kuliang in the mountains near Foochow

Two important developments in the province took place that year. First, instead of being part of the Diocese of Southern China, based in Hong Kong, Fukien became a separate diocese with its own Bishop in Foochow. The appointment of Bishop Price to this position had already been announced in the first edition of the *Foochow Church Gazette*, a new dual language magazine.[27] This restructuring would provide more empathetic pastoral and administrative support.

Second, the Republican movement pressing for the overthrow of the Qing Dynasty was beginning to grow in strength. Its leader, Sun-Yat-sen, had been influenced by Western ideals and Christian beliefs, and its core principles were nationalism, democracy, and socialism. Although strongest in the south of the country, particularly around Canton, the movement was beginning to extend its influence northward and gain more adherents among students and educated Chinese.[28]

---

27. *Foochow Church Gazette*, vol. 1, 1906, 1.
28. Schiffrin, *Sun Yat-sen*, ch.2.

4

Striving for Reform as the "Sleeping Dragon" Awakes

THE FIRST TEN YEARS, the saying goes, are the hardest! Early 1907 marked a decade since Sophie had arrived in China. On reflection, many challenges had been tackled—developing a new mission with two other women in a community dominated by men; finding resources to develop female education; countering the force of superstition that prevented understanding of their message; having to evacuate the district for a protracted time; confronting the effects of natural disasters and plagues; and the falling away of some who had been baptized. At the personal level, periodic migraines reducing her capacity to study and work had been lessened due to medical care.

On occasions, she felt disheartened, especially when comparing the situation with what was happening through CIM in other parts of the country. Earlier she had written:

> This seems a very dismal letter, but I have written it hurriedly, and it is but the expression of what has been growing on me for a long time. As I read of God's work in Inland China, and in other parts of the world, in our periodicals, I cannot think they would be saying the same.[1]

---

1. S. S. Newton, Annual Letter, 13 December 1904, 2. The mention of "inland China" refers to the work of Hudson Taylor and the CIM, whose story is told in Taylor, *China Inland Mission*, vol. 2.

Despite many obstacles, Sophie had seen signs of God's presence and influence. "It is not all dark, I am thankful to say. There are a few bright spots in individual cases, for which we praise God."[2]

In the following period, the muted tone of some of her letters began to change. Her work was moving into a more overtly productive phase, in some respects mirroring positive changes that were appearing more openly in the society around her. The "sleeping dragon," as some portrayed China, was stirring into life through new groups and forces emerging in the country. This was not merely a coincidence, for in certain areas there was a symbiosis between religious and civic concerns. Partly for this reason, it is mostly more helpful to describe Sophie's work via a few key themes rather than as, up to now, in chronological sequence. The most relevant themes are direct evangelism, female education, girls, status, and drug prevention.

梁劉柔芬

The first of these, *direct evangelism*, remained high on Sophie's agenda. The challenge was not just to convince villagers and city-dwellers that idols did not exist and were unable to protect, guide, or improve their lives. It meant persuading them to give up the many superstitious devices they used to fend off their dread of evil spirits. They put tiger's heads on children's bibs and shoes to keep the spirits at bay. Nets were made and placed over their clothes, as well as windows and doors, to entangle the spirits. Boys were often given girls names to deceive them, as they did not think spirits thought girls were worth bothering about.[3]

Even though the mission was short-staffed with Minna still away on furlough, Sophie cleared time to undertake evangelism elsewhere. Leaving the Girls School in the capable hands of a pupil-teacher, she was sometimes able to get away for a week to instruct a class of enquirers. Her account of one of these visits is quite descriptive.

> I spent several weeks in another part of the district, a lovely spot on the foot of a hill on the shore of a beautiful bay. Over 20 women came regularly every day to learn, and it was good to see how they responded to the teaching; several had rather mixed motives in coming but they seemed to quietly withdraw. I am much cheered

---

2. S. S. Newton, Annual Letter, 27 November 1905, 2.

3. This draws on Isobel Suttor's description that was reported in Sophie's former home town's *Mudgee Guardian & Northwestern Representative*, 21 October 1909, 16.

and believe that precious souls were saved during that visit. It has hitherto been a most hard and difficult village to visit, but now one finds real pleasure in going there.[4]

On another occasion, she spent "a very positive time" over several weeks with around thirty women, a number of whom were inquirers, some preparing for baptism, and others for confirmation.[5]

The following year, Sophie made a change in her usual patterns of evangelism in Deng-doi. She decided to replace time-consuming house-to-house visiting among inquirers with a station class to which those interested were invited. Making this the standard approach to conducting local outreach also cleared more time to follow up believers in the villages around the city.

It also gave more time to advance the work among well-to-do women in the city itself. From her previous experience, she had developed a modus operandi for reaching the women on whom they were focusing. In most cases, it was best for one of her existing contacts to provide an introduction. Once inside, finer points of etiquette had to be observed to avoid being regarded as a barbarian. As part of this, time had to be allowed for considerable small talk before more serious matters in life could be raised. This could include being asked quite private questions such as: Why are your feet so large? Who bought your dull dress? Why do you not have black hair? Why are you not married? Once there was opportunity to tell something of her life story, it was possible to share how the gospel came into it. All this took time, especially as cultural differences meant that most Chinese women took a long time to begin understanding the basics of Christianity, let alone embrace them.

From the beginning, a commitment to *female education* lay at the heart of Sophie's work in Deng-doi. This took various forms and she now sought to develop each of these further. At the basic level, she helped consolidate the training of young women to serve the growing numbers of children attending Sunday School. This was mainly done through extending the adult Bible Study she superintended from just one group studying a particular biblical book to several groups meeting to study different Old or New Testament books at the same time.

While the Qing Government's recent reforms introduced new schools, it largely maintained the limited type of students who could attend, teaching

---

4. S. S. Newton, Annual Letter, 26 November 1907, 1.
5. S. S. Newton, Annual Letter, 26 November 1907, 1.

in classical rather than vernacular Chinese, and sidelined all but a minute number of girls.[6] This meant schools established by Christians remained the only ones catering to female education. The senior girl who sometimes taught in her place in Deng-doi, Hung Ong, would go on to train full-time at the Teacher's Training College in Foochow. When opportunity arose, Sophie was fond of telling everyone that China's daughters were well worth training, and could excel in becoming nurses, teachers, and doctors.

Freeing married women to attend the three-month long course at the Women's School remained a continuing challenge. Husbands generally regarded their wives as solely available to meet their needs and look after children. The favorite description of their spouses in China was the "one at the back of the house." For Sophie, persuading them otherwise was mostly an ongoing, one-by-one, time-consuming, challenge. Doing this remained high on her agenda as, for her, the Women's School was the most important responsibility. Its informal, residential, down-to-earth approach gave it a special character. In the first term of 1908, she decided to move out of the missionary house so she could live for three months with incoming students at the school. Looking back on this experience, she wrote:

> a great many crowded into the five rooms, and God made his presence felt, and that roused the enemy, so that it in some ways it was a hard term. Still, as I look back, I can see that much worked for good. Living with them, while it is not easy to get accustomed to the noise, at the same time one gets to know the women better.[7]

As the original building was no longer large enough to house it, more rooms were added to accommodate thirty to forty participants. Unfortunately, in 1908 the Matron of the School suddenly died, and it took Sophie a long time to search among the Christians in the district for a replacement.

Though not wishing to overturn long-standing Chinese traditions unnecessarily, in two respects *girls status* was a particular concern. One of these was parents' arranging marriages of young girls to older men for financial gain. When women taught in Sophie's school became Christian, they she occasionally asked her to persuade their non-Christian husbands to refrain from this practice.

---

6. Sally Borthwick, *Schooling and Society*, 152–79.
7. S. S. Newton, Annual Letter, 25 November 1908, 1.

An example of the horrific effects of foot-binding

Another concern was the severely painful custom of foot-binding infant girls, except for poorer ones who had to work in the fields, to increase their marriage prospects and consequent financial value. According to a familiar Chinese proverb, "A woman who has the long legs ends up alone in a room." Having small feet was considered a mark of beauty, sexual allure, and fertility. For some time, protests against this physically abusive, horribly painful practice had surfaced in some quarters of Chinese society.[8] The first anti-foot binding society had been formed in Shanghai thirty years earlier and, at the turn of the century, some magistrates, Confucian, and Buddhist leaders started a new movement opposed to this practice was initiated. A

8. See further Bossen, Laurel, and Hill Gates. *Bound Feet, Young Hands.*

further ally in this was the forming of a National Foot Society in the first session of the reform-minded Fujian Provincial Assembly. This was partly through the influence of a number of Protestant Chinese Christian members who were resolutely opposed to foot-binding.[9]

A final issue claiming the women's attention, *drug prevention*, was an offshoot of their medical work. They actively sought women converts to help their husbands give up opium and squandering their wages in dens. Sophie and her colleagues were encouraged by the formation of an Anti-Opium Society by scholar-officials in Foochow which was authorized to treat addicts and confiscate the drug. When, to celebrate its first anniversary, a city-wide parade against opium was orgianzed, missionaries actively supported it. Attracting over ten thousand people, the largest crowd outside a festival in the city's history, this led to public burnings of the drug and the closing of more than three thousand opium dens.[10]

Anti-Opium League public meeting in Lieng Kong

9. Dunch, *Fuzhou Protestants*, 86.
10. Faith-Davies, "Anti-Footbinding, 116–19; and Dunch, *Fuzhou Protestants*, 49–55.

After this, the Society began to extend its work into rural areas, including the district of Lieng Kong, and worked to clamp down on farmers suspected of growing crops of opium. A public meeting was held in a temple in the city, attended by mandarins, city elders, missionaries, school teachers, and a large crowd. Sophie was invited on to the Speaker's Platform along with a CMS clergyman, the local pastor, city leader, a distinguished lady, and delegates from the Anti-Opium Society. She spoke from her first-hand experience of meeting with people who were caught in the drug's vicious web or thrown into poverty by its effects, as well as the positive help available from the mission's medical treatment, community support, and spiritual renewal.

The following evening, at the request of the city elders, the missionaries joined in a discussion of practical ways to work against opium addiction. This led to opening opium-curing establishments, sending deputations throughout the district, visitation of every house in the city, and posting up the names of opium makers. This was the first time the city elders had anything to do with our church.

As a result of the meeting, a district branch of the Anti-Opium Society was formed. The Qing Government also finally enacted plans to suppress the cultivation of opium and prevent its importation. Regrettably, the British Government exerted its extensive power to preserve opium exports at ten percent, and in response the Chinese Government decided to only lessen rather than prohibit local production. At the time, Sophie was concerned about both over-zealous attempts to eradicate addiction that failed to help victims withdraw from it, as well as underwhelming responses by those primarily interested in limiting their economic losses with inadequate concern for how it was destroying lives.

> As far as the opium suppression goes, we still feel that 'hope deferred makes the heart grow sick.' While much is being done there is not the wise vigilance and tact necessary to suppress it gradually not entirely. Sometimes the reformers are so severe [as] to be cruel, at other times so lenient that they wink at it all. But what is to be done when it still pours in from India? If only England would be able to help Christians as she alone can! We do feel so ashamed when asked if it is not England who trades in opium?"[11]

---

11. S. Newton, Annual Letter, 30 November, 1908, 1. Missionary opposition in China to the opium trade is explored in Lodwick, *Crusaders Against Opium* Kentucky, 1996.

An additional area about which the women missionaries could do little to address directly was the abandoning of baby girls in so-called deposit boxes or baby towers. Unlike boys, who would grow up to engage in productive, money-making work, girls were regarded as basically a financial liability who had to be supported. Their basic value was that, as parents aged and became dependent, it would be helpful to have one who could care for them and look after the house. Although one day they would marry and might attract a reasonable dowry, finding a well-to-do husband for them was very uncertain and, apart from bringing a one-off financial advantage, involved further expenditure on hiring a marriage-broker. Because of the secrecy involved in such activities, Sophie and her co-workers could not do anything to physically prevent them. All they could do was seek to argue against the practice in various classes and informal discussions.

Typical baby-tower in rural Fukien

In the last annual letter before her second furlough in early 1909, Sophie noted two developments that were prescient for the mission's future. Under Nellie Marshall's effective work in the Dispensary, numbers had now grown significantly, further underscoring the need for a hospital and a doctor. It made more sense to do this in a larger center like Lieng Kong city. Secondly, Minna Searle had decided to find rented premises outside the West Gate of that city to further her work among higher-status women there. Since, as earlier in Foochow, there was still some suspicion of foreigners residing within the city's walls, she found a place just outside these.[12] Though the little band of missionaries in Lieng Kong—now numbering four with Marion Onyon from the UK doing language study—did not know it, this was a step towards ultimately transferring their headquarters to the provincial capital. Though she did not mention it, a significant political development that took place in November that year was the death of the Empress Dowager who had reigned for so long and, the following day, the boy Emperor who would have replaced her. This increased uncertainty about China's future in a fast-modernizing world.[13]

梁劉柔芬

The only long break Sophie had during her second term in Fukien was a trip in the summer of 1907 via Shanghai to Japan with two missionary friends.[14] It was six years since her previous visit, and she enjoyed exploring the sights in Kobe and elsewhere. The highlight was a trip to a mountain retreat at Karvizaw, ninety miles north-west from Tokyo. In this lovely, quiet spot, the three friends spent time in fellowship with God and one another. They made a lifelong "covenant" to pray regularly for one another, as well as "pledging" to prioritize "faithfulness" in their missionary call.

Sophie's second furlough fell eighteen months later. While she was eager to see family and friends again back home, it was especially hard to leave Daik-hok and Ai-co. On 27 January she sailed for Hong Kong. Transiting there for a week during Chinese New Year, she was eager to meet up with two of Robert and Louisa Stewart's children who had briefly met when they visited Foochow a year earlier. She had mentioned then their father's impact upon her life during his visit to Australia, but was keen to see how their work was developing. In Hong Kong she was able to hear Arthur preach at St Paul's Chinese church which he had founded only a few weeks before. Unfortunately, her ship was due to leave just two days

---

12. S. S. Newton, Annual Letter, 30 November 1908, 1–2.

13. Despite her support of the Boxer Uprising, the Empress's contribution to the modernizing of the country is explored in Chang, *Dowager Empress Cixi*.

14. Sophie does not mention their surnames, but they appear to be (Dr) Mabel Hanington and Margaret Boileau, who most probably nursed her during a migraine episode. Even though Mabek was Canadian, both had gone out with British CMS. A helpful summary of the role of female UK missionaries in the country occurs in Delia Davin, "British Women Missionaries, 257–71.

before the official opening of St Paul's Boys School with him as Principal and Kathleen as a teacher.[15]

Leaving Hong Kong on 3 February, she arrived in Sydney exactly three weeks later. Initially, she spent special time with her mother Emma as well as her sister Grace who was now Matron of a major Christian high school in Sydney. Then came deputations in churches and Christian organizations throughout the city and state, for which she usually dressed in Chinese clothes and brought exhibits from Lieng Kong.

On occasions, there were significant conversations with individuals about her work in China. One of these was with a relative in the coastal town of Nowra, a half days travel from Sydney.

> My cousin was very interested and asked what it would cost to keep a girl in school for a year and I told her about two pounds, ten shillings, covering two terms of four months each. [I thought of] a bright girl, daughter of our Chinese teacher, to be the one supported...Her name was Hung Ong meaning 'Grace'. She is a very clever girl, about 12, and the first to enter the school, very capable in every way, and a born leader. She was head of the school each term and in many subjects received 100 marks![16]

During her furlough, Sophie was wrestling with two spiritual issues. These were not matters of belief but of practice, one connected with the church and the other with the mission. The first two of Sophie's surviving journals, whose chief aim was to provide "an account of God's dealing with his child" over this period and allow us to enter more fully into her concerns.

---

15. Their story, and that of their siblings, is told in our book *Children of the Massacre*.
16. Address to CMA Supporters in Nowra, CMS Archives Australia, 1909, undated.

> March 19 1908 Feel I must just put down in this second little note book a word of praise to God for stirring my soul up for a life of more perfect love & faith, & how much I do thank Him for these longings, & better still for the assurance that I am all for God, & cleansed from all sin, & that it is by faith alone in the precious blood. I am going on unto perfection by the grace of God. He has lovingly put into my hands the life of Carvosso. I feel I must copy out a few lines from seq. on page 208. He speaks of Lady Maxwell's life being such a help to him, & copies from her book the following: "From day to day I am made to taste of that perfect love wh casts out fear; & often I experience a pleni-

Sample page from Sophie's second journal, 1908–1910

For several months before returning home, she had been wondering about the validity of her baptism as an infant. This began after attending an adult baptism in the church at Deng-doi, when some women and a few male converts were fully immersed. This was a big step of faith, not just for them but because it is such a public statement before their families, village—even their ancestors! In comparison, her baptism seemed rather insignificant. Shortly after, she read how the missioner George Grubb, though christened as an infant, felt he should follow Christ's example and be baptized by immersion. In reading over relevant biblical passages, she was struck by how baptism was portrayed in connection with Paul and even Jesus himself![17]

Though not sure what all this meant, especially as a member of the Anglican church, in the next few months Sophie took several steps to explore it further. She talked it over with two non-Anglican missionary friends who had taken this step, wrote to various people including George Grubb whose opinion she respected, and reading some materials on the issue by people on both sides of the debate. Despite all this, she could not reach any definite conclusion. Shortly after, however, a letter came from one of the two friends who had been baptized by immersion. While not regretting her decision to do so, in retrospect this friend felt she had made too much of it. Her advice, which came to Sophie like "a voice from God" was to ensure you only suffered for Christ, not for a sacrament.

The second issue arose from knowing that some people went to the mission field without any regular salary, simply relying on God to provide for their needs. Her first knowledge of this had come from reading about Hudson Taylor, and learning that this was how colleagues in the China Inland Mission were expected to operate.[18] Though she was aware that CMA's policy was apportioning everyone a salary out of money that came in, this ran the risk of taking God's provision for granted and lessening their dependence on Him. Was God now calling her to a further step in this direction for all her financial needs? If so, would this not jeopardize her relationship with CMA and therefore serving in Lieng Kong?

Despite seeking and learning about others' experience, Sophie increasingly found working through these issues a lonely affair. A poem she came across around this time, caught her feelings exactly:

> There is a mystery in human hearts:
> And though we be encircled by a host
> Of those who love us well, and are beloved,
> To every one of us, from time to time,
> There comes a sense of utter loneliness...
> "There is not one who *really* understands,

---

17. Though Sophie had not undertaken academic study, her instincts in this matter were in line with contemporary biblical scholarship, as Jeremias, *Origins of Infant Baptism*, demonstrates. For my brief summary of Paul's view, see Banks, *Paul's Idea of Community*, 67–69.

18. This was the fourth of CIM's fifteen basic missionary precepts. See further H. H. Rowden, " Concept of Living by Faith"; and Fiedler, *Story of Faith Missions*, 32.

Not one to enter into *all* I feel."
Such is the cry of each of us in turn;
We enter into "a solitary way."[19]

The poem went on to propose that the reason for this was Christ's desire to be the *key* person at such a time. This deeply appealed to her, though the further idea that He should be not just the key but *only* person to satisfy someone in such situations, fitted more with her tendency to reflect a more mystical version of Keswick piety.

After much time thinking and praying this whole matter over, Sophie decided this was a step God wanted her to take. Knowing that, except for a very few with a private income, CMA's policy was to pay all their missionaries from a central fund, Sophie assumed this meant resigning. A final word from God came to her in the words of Isaiah: "You have not passed this way heretofore." (3:4) While it was heart-wrenching to write to the Association, the part that:

> "... hurt most is leaving Lieng Kong and my beloved companions, and all the workers, and all those dear associations, and yet He is almighty. He might even yet bring it about—at any rate in a matter of this kind we dare not, we must not, look at things that can be seen, only Him whom we serve and must follow, though it may be a new, untrodden, and untried way.[20]

Writing further letters to family, friends, and colleagues, took a whole night. Then, like a dream, just as God provided Abraham a way out as he was offering up his firstborn son Isaac (Genesis 22), there came an unexpected alternative. After several interviews with members of the CMA Committee, she received a formal letter saying that they unanimously wished her to continue with them and agreed to a special arrangement regarding support. Reading this, the words that accompanied her initial dedication to missionary service came again: "Delight thyself in the Lord, and He will fulfil all the desires of thy heart" (Psalm 37:4). The only negative note was hearing later that CMS missionaries in Kuliang had not reacted well to her decision when word spread about it at their summer conference.

梁劉柔芬

---

19. "A Solitary Way", 1.
20. S. S. Newton, Second Journal, 26 January 1909.

During the last six months of her furlough, Sophie had the opportunity to share with two groups that were especially important to her. One was the annual NSW Church Missionary Association Convention in the Blue Mountains outside Sydney. This gathering of missionaries on furlough, others about to leave to the mission field, and dedicated supporters of the Society was held in a large country-style house overlooking the expansive Jamison Valley. She was given the important responsibility of speaking at the Valedictory Service for those heading overseas.

Another special occasion was addressing staff and students at Deaconess House in Sydney. This reminded Sophie of the time training for mission work at Louisa Hassall's Marsden Home, the predecessor to this larger institution. There, drawing on her fifteen-year experience in the field, she spoke about the spiritual struggle against shallowness, renewing allegiance to Christ, victory over sin, and healing through the atonement.[21]

On 3 August 1910 Sophie boarded the SS *Eastern* again for Hong Kong. Ten days into the voyage, however, the ship became grounded on a mudbank as it was being piloted into the port of Rockhampton in Queensland. It was stuck there for eleven days, during which Sophie began suffering from migraines. When the boat arrived in Hong Kong, though still troubled by headaches, on her birthday she attended St John's Cathedral, receiving an encouraging word from God through Bishop Lander's scripture reading and sermon.

On reaching Foochow in mid-September, Sophie went first to Tak-Ding Hospital, and was then able to spend time first with Mabel for three days on the island of Sharp Peak, at the mouth of the Min River, and then on Sunday with Maggie in Foochow. On her return to Deng-doi, knowing that she might never have come back there, meeting up with Daik-Hok and Ai-cio, as well as her colleagues, Chinese fellow-workers, and local Christians, was deeply moving. To her delight, Daik-hok was doing extremely well at Trinity College, and she hoped that he might follow in the footsteps of her father, John Newton, to study medicine and become a doctor.

Sophie was eager to resume her work in the district again. In the area of *direct evangelism*, further moves were taking place to relocate the base of the mission's outreach to the city of Lieng Kong. Minna had made her

---

21. The latter two topics were characteristic of a minority approach in the Keswick Movement that was more in accord with Wesleyan rather than Anglican perspectives. This should not be confused, however, with the more extreme view known as "sinless perfectionism." One of the books Sophie read was Andrew Murray, *The Holiest of All*, 1894.

temporary rental of premises permanent, and Nellie was making plans to build a Dispensary for people in the town.

In the area of *female education*, the new Girls' Boarding School Sophie had opened in Deng-doi before she left on furlough had now grown to thirty students. The school's first graduate to have trained at the Teacher's Training College in Foochow, wanted to return to her old school and Sophie appointed her as its first Chinese Headmistress. Her thoughts now turned to setting up a Girls Boarding School in the district capital. The desire to transfer the Womens School there also strengthened her plans to make Lieng Kong a full-time base.

In the area of *girls status*, the women missionaries in Lieng Kong had framed a policy of only accepting girls into schools if parents unbound their feet. This initiative was a major advance in dealing with the problem, and compliance with it had increased when it received support from the authorities in Foochow.

In the area of *drug prevention*, greater suppression of opium and closing of dens led to larger numbers of men turning up at the Dispensary to deal with the symptoms of withdrawal. In one of her furlough addresses, Sophie had talked about this "curse" and that many dozens "of 'opium-slaves' had been saved by taking them to their dispensaries, and tearfully tending" them.[22]

In such matters, it is sometimes difficult to judge how much the actions of missionaries were motivated by their Western values or by their specifically Christian beliefs? Complicating this question is the extent to which Western values had themselves been shaped over the centuries by Christian attitudes. In any case, in evangelical circles at the time there was a strong link between basic Christian convictions and active compassion towards the poor and disadvantaged. What we do know from the writings of Sophie and her co-workers is that they viewed opposing foot-binding and opium addiction as a requirement of living in a Christ-like way.

---

22. *Singleton Argus,* Saturday 19 June 1909, 4.

STRIVING FOR REFORM AS THE "SLEEPING DRAGON" AWAKES

Imposing West Gate of Lieng Kong City

Since a key way forward in all these areas was moving their base of operations from the village of Deng-doi to the city of Lieng Kong, finding the most suitable place for this was the prime concern. Sophie and her co-workers were hoping to find a site on the less densely settled land outside the West Gate which was near the main river route to inland or coastal villages. In the spring of 1911, a spacious walled plot with some buildings that could immediately be put into use and room for others that would need to be constructed became available for a very modest price. This was provided by Mrs Ahok, the first well-known woman evangelist in the province who had also addressed meetings overseas. She had been a friend and colleague of the Stewarts before their deaths fifteen years earlier.[23] A detailed description of the site was provided by Minna Searle.

> We are so very thankful that at last the way has opened up for premises to be purchased just outside the city, where it is hoped that before long permanent work may be established. It is a charming spot, and was purchased for 'a mere song', so we are full of thankfulness, and looking forward to the work developing in several directions. A new dispensary is to be built immediately, and later on, we trust, a Girls Boarding School, as we

---

23. The role of Mrs Ahok occurs in the Annual Report, New South Wales Church Missionary Association, 1909–1910, 11. On her connection with the Stewarts, see our book *Children of the Massacre*. More fully on Mrs Ahok, see Barnes, *Behind the Great Wall*, 60–90.

have the land available and funds in hand for building. The inner compound, where the present buildings are, has a very pretty entrance, surrounded by fruit trees and shrubs, and entered by large double doors, over which are seen the characters 'Ang', 'Loc', 'Ga' (Peace, Happiness, Home), in deep blue coloring which looks very effective. Passing through these doors, we are confronted with a quaint-looking red building, the servants' quarters, which has a large native guest-hall elaborately decorated with handsome carvings of various devices—dragons, fish, lotus flowers, and so on. The coloring of these decorations is delightful, having been toned down by age.

Turning round a little to the right, attention is at once arrested by a still more attractive two-storey building, i.e., the Ladies' House. The turned-up roof, with its wide-spreading eaves, supported at each corner by a huge carved butterfly, and the balcony roof adorned with four grotesque-looking creatures of the canine order, together with prettily tinted carved blossoms of different kinds gives the place an oriental look; but the main part of the building is in foreign style, with a great many windows and is beautifully cool and airy. Leaving this we pass through the rustic gate of a low wall that separates the rest of the compound from what the Chinese call a 'gar sang' (a play mountain), or what we call 'a fancy garden', a wonderful place of rugged moss-grown rocks, lots of ferns and shrubs with queer little winding passages and stone stairways: an ideal spot for children to play.

In the midst of this stands the building which has been adapted and added to for a Women's School. This school will probably be in full swing when this account is printed. So may I take the opportunity of soliciting much earnest prayer on behalf of these dear women, that God's Word may find an entrance and bring light and life to every soul in the school.[24]

梁劉柔芬

While the women from Deng-doi were settling into their new premises and finalizing plans for the next stage if their work in the district, other changes were taking place in the country at large that were to decisively influence the future shape of their work. These had their tangible beginnings in Sun-Yat-sen's rise to power in Canton mentioned at the end of the last chapter. In the following period, hopes of gaining wider support

---

24. *Church Missionary Gleaner*, September 1911, 137–38.

for this movement to transform China into a more democratic Republic failed to materialize. In the last few months of the year, however, a series of events took place that, more quickly than anyone expected, built momentum for radical change.

This began in late summer in the province of Sichuan, West China, where resentment had been building against the Qing Dynasty for some time. An underground League, comprised of a wide range of citizens, started to organize open resistance against the Central Government and its local Viceroy in the cultural capital of Chengtu. Mainly directed at the Dynasty's tardiness in modernizing the country, and refusal to give more power to regional governments, this was in sympathy with Sun-Yat-sen's campaign for national reform. Though the resistance movement was not opposed to the presence and work of missionaries, the Viceroy ordered them to gather in the capital and evacuate to another province.

The resistance turned into an uprising that soon spread elsewhere in Sichuan, and one after another cities capitulated, including the provincial capital, Chungking. In early autumn, a military rebellion then arose in Wuchang, central China, that had a ripple effect on other regional military bases along the Yangtze River, such as Hankow, known as "little Shanghai." Meanwhile, Sun-Yat-sen was encouraged to return from overseas where he had been gathering support and funding for his cause.[25] In Fujian, forces in support of or opposed to the republican movement vied for supremacy in the most populated eastern parts of the province. While the capital, Foochow, was a main crucible of conflict, Lieng Kong city lay directly on the main north-south route traveled by soldiers in the country.

---

25. For more detail on these developments, see Hsu, *Rise of Modern China*, 466–70.

5

A New Republic Stirs up the Winds of Change

WHILE PROVINCIAL AUTHORITIES IN Foochow were supportive of the Nationalist revolution, the army remained faithful to the Imperial government. Less than forty miles away in their mission station, the little band of sisters "retired to bed at night not knowing what was going to happen the next day."[1] For Sophie, this feeling was heightened by a visit from Daik-hok. Instead of completing teacher training in Foochow College, wanted to give priority to his growing patriotism and join the armed struggle against the Qing dynasty. Before doing this, he had come to ask her blessing on his resolve. Though Sophie was concerned that he would be putting himself in harm's way, she endorsed his love of country, asking him only to continue putting love to God first.

In early November, soldiers sympathetic to the republican cause staged an uprising in the city. A day-long battle began near the North Gate, spread along the city's main street and ended in surrender by most of the Qing forces. The Provincial Government declared itself in favor of the revolution, one of the first in the country to do so. Its Protestant members, including the the Vice-President, the Secretary, and the Chairman of the Executive Committee, actively supported this move.[2]

---

1. This comes from a letter of Minna Searle reported in the *Hobart Mercury*, 1 March 1912, 6.
2. In Dunch, *Fuzhou Protestants*, 112–22, the author provides a detailed account of the provincial Government response to the republican cause before, during, and after its

Sophie was relieved to hear that Daik-hok was safe. One evening a little later, the CMS women in Lieng Kong heard that some Imperial Government soldiers were retreating towards the city and intended to make their mission compound their place of refuge. The next morning, around one hundred armed men from surrounding villages appeared, broke down the gate, and massed before the Ladies House, affirming their willingness to defend it. As it happened, the retreating Imperial forces never materialized. When the Republican Army took the city and raised the revolutionary flag, one of its first actions was to offer the missionaries protection against not only opposing soldiers but looters and bandits in the area.

A few days before Christmas, uprisings against the Qing Dynasty throughout China culminated in the so-called Xinhai Revolution leading to the abdication of Puyi, the boy Emperor. On 1 January 1912, China was declared a Republic, Nanking was declared the new capital, and Sun Yat-sen was elected provisional President.[3]

The new President's sympathy toward Christianity and promise of wider religious toleration, were welcomed by the missionaries in Fukien. The new government immediately began to introduce laws affecting areas of Chinese society. One of the most symbolic was abolishing the mandatory wearing of queues by males. These marks of subservience to those with higher status no longer had a place. In cities like Lieng Kong, most males cut off their pigtails, but in villages like Deng-doi the majority of men found this too radical. In cities, educated men and some women also began to dress more in Western than Chinese style.

For a time, resistance to the Republic occasionally surfaced. In Foochow, a bomb explosion endangered the life of the new civil governor and there were occasional threats against Christian institutions. Three months after taking office, Sun Yat-sen stood down in favor of General Yuan Shi-kai, who had been promised the Presidency if he brought about surrender of the last Qing supporters. Sun himself focused on creating the Kuomintang, or National People's Party, as a further step towards a fully elected democratic system. Later that year, he visited Foochow to thank the city for its support of the new Republic during the revolution.[4]

---

national victory.

3. The history of the events leading up to and beyond founding of the Republic is told by Lary, *China's Republic*, 11–80.

4. Dunch, *Fuzhou Protestants*, 65, 123, 128.

靈光盲學校

Among the reforms the new regime instituted were adding more Day Schools for boys and starting Day Schools for girls; building new Hospitals and Dispensaries; banning the customs of infant betrothals and foot-binding; outlawing the practice of female infanticide; and calling for an end of the opium trade. These were generally welcomed, drawing only minor criticism in the countryside when they affected Chinese religious traditions. Overall, there was little reaction to the widespread destruction of idols when temples were transformed into schools.

Government support of female education encouraged the Lieng Kong mission to establish a Day School for girls in the city. With the consent of the local pastor, a Chinese catechist had started a new church in the hospital chapel for people living outside the West Gate. Since evangelism and discipleship in the wider district were increasingly being taken over by graduates of the Women's School, both Minna Searle and Marion Onyon were freed to work more in the district capital. Under Nellie Marshall, the Dispensary was drawing more patients not only from surrounding villages but from within the city walls.

Hospital and dispensary in Lieng Kong mission

Her leadership position in the district capital resulted in Sophie becoming a member of the Diocese of Fukien's Educational Committee. Early in 1912, this met in Foochow to decide how its schools could best support the new government initiatives. Clara Lambert, Principal of the CMS Girls School in the capital, wanted to propose that Foochow Normal School develop a teacher training program for graduates from missionary as well as government schools. Sophie, seeing the potential for students from the Girls School in Lieng Kong, was strongly in favor.

This decade was the start of what was called "the golden age" of Protestant influence in early modern China.[5] It also marked the end of the seventy-five years long trade in opium, as on 7 May 1913, the British Government officially announced its termination. Unfortunately, this victory for Chinese sovereignty, was offset by the beginning of President Yuan Shikei's retreat from some key Republican principles. His efforts to centralize power in his own hands resulted in a gradual decline in the Central Government's influence as local warlords began to re-assert their influence.

Though authorities in Foochow continued to support the government in Nanking, they were concerned that opposition to it would grow and that it might generate more bandit groups increasing raids in the province. To forestall these, they stationed troops in Lieng Kong and a few of the larger villages, including Deng-doi. The CMS Secretary of the Fukien Mission visited the city's Church Council in early March and wrote about

> the encouraging fact that the meetings were attended by the military officers in charge of the soldiers stationed in the city, one of whom has been a regular attendant at our services for some time, and who seems to be in earnest. He has had intercourse with missionaries for a long time . . . and prepared an elaborate feast for me . . . his brother officer, our native clergyman, and catechist . . .
>
> The next morning I went by boat to Deng-doi, where . . . one of the [officers there] attended the church in Deng-doi on two or three occasions, and seemed very favorably disposed towards Christianity. In the evening I walked back to Lieng Kong, and there found an invitation to dine with one of the wealthiest families in the city, who have lately joined the Church . . . [and] are not far from the Kingdom of Heaven . . .[6]

---

5. There is a definitive treatment of this in Bays, *A New History*, 92–120 and, specifically in Fukien, Dunch, *Fuzhou Protestants*, 148–77.

6. *Church Missionary Gleaner*, May 1913, 380.

This incident opens a small window into the way Christianity was gradually making inroads into both civic and military circles in the district.

By summer, it was clear that the strenuous demands of the past year had taken a toll on Sophie's health. This situation was compounded by an unusually severe cholera outbreak in the district that resulted in many deaths. Sophie recorded that:

> Two of our little school girls died while we were away. One . . . a dear child . . . When ill her mother went to ask the idols what medicine to give her, but she refused to take it, and clenched her teeth so that they could not force it down her throat . . . Our teacher's wife died after a few hours illness. Miss Marshall was with her, but it was hopeful from the first. The teacher was at Kuliang, and walked home half the day and through the night, but she was buried by the time he reached the house. His daughter also caught it but recovered and so did another girl who was in the Boarding School . . .

Fortunately, Sophie's adoptive ward, Ai-cio, did not catch cholera and, after Hung Ong left for Teacher Training College in Foochow, her cousin and friends in Australia indicated that they would like their support to be directed to her. The young girl was, as a letter to them noted, turning into a caring as well as studious girl.

> I was looking over her wardrobe to see what she needed as I paid for her clothes and missed a warm coat and asked where it was, and found she had given it to a *very* poor girl about her own age as she had two and could spare it. It was well deserved and I noticed those two became great friends even after they were married.[7]

---

7. S. S. Newton, "Letter to Supporters in Nowra," Banks Family Collection.

Decorated entrance of Lieng Kong Mission compound

The heavy demands missionaries faced during this time led to CMS advising Sophie, and a few others, to go on furlough earlier than planned. In late December, after preparing missionary colleagues and Chinese workers in Lieng Kong for her absence, she stood on the balcony of the Ladies House to survey how far the mission compound had developed in the last three years. To her immediate right was a small, originally rocky, area, that she had lovingly turned into a terraced garden growing some of her favorite Chinese vegetables and flowers. Looking down the walled area on the right side of the compound she dwelt for a while on the two-storey Women's School with its upstairs dormitory and downstairs classrooms, refectory, and kitchen. In the far-right corner itself was a small residence for the school Principal and, along the bottom wall, the Girls Boarding School. This was where young Ai-cio was now old enough to become a student. Looking back up the wall from the far left-hand corner were the Hospital, Dispensary and Chapel. Half-way along the wall, a pathway from the Entrance Gate led to the Worker's Quarters for the watchman, cook, catechist, and a nurse. Adjacent to this was a Chinese style Guest Hall, where inquirers could come to drink tea and listen to Bible stories or Christian songs. Beyond this, leading up to her residence was room for an additional building, such as a church. In the center of the complex was a grassed area where children could play and adults relax. When filled with adults and children, the complex felt like the heart of a small village. Sophie took great pleasure from the fact that, though outside one of its Gates, it was increasingly regarded as an extension of the city, and as a hub of the surrounding villages.

靈光盲學校

On 9 January, Sophie said goodbye to Lieng Kong to spend two weeks in Foochow before sailing to Hong Kong. The next day she boarded the *SS Aldenham* for Australia, arriving in Sydney in late February. Her arrival was reported in the main city newspaper under the headline "Return of a Missionary."[8]

During her furlough, she spoke in many venues throughout Sydney and NSW. Though the subjects of these talks varied, they mainly focused on the challenge of Christianity to Chinese religious beliefs and practice, as well as its impact on the lives and roles of women in her district. An innovative idea that surfaced during one of her visits was churches setting up reading circles in homes so women could keep in touch with missionary work and pray for it. In early August, her schedule was interrupted by the disturbing news that England and Germany were at war and, since Australia was part of the British Empire, that it was also at war. She knew this could involve members of her wider family, affect local churches, and possibly disrupt mission work. Though China was not involved in any way, however, she assumed that returning and staying there would not be an issue.

In early 1915, she received a copy of a letter from Minna describing recent Christmas celebrations in the mission complex which also provided a vibrant sense of what was happening in the work at Lieng Kong more generally.

---

8. In the Shipping News column of *Sydney Morning Herald*, 26 February 1914.

We were unfortunate in our Christmas weather this year, as it poured in torrents all the day and night before, and almost without a break on Christmas Day itself. It was very disappointing, especially for the Catechists in the different churches [in the district], as so few could get to the services. The church in the city was so prettily decorated, and looked very bright and festive, but none of our women or girls could get over to the service, so we had to content ourselves with having worship in the Hospital chapel in the compound . . . However, the wet weather did not seem to affect the happiness of these who joined in the festivities here, and we had a very happy, though rather full, day. Breakfast and Prayers over, we all went to the Girls' School for their Christmas Tree, which was very gay with your many nice gifts. The happiness of the children would have made all we have worked so hard feel rewarded for their kindness and trouble, I same sure . . . we then repaired to the chapel for a bright Christmas service; then dinner. We had great doings in the afternoon, though part of the programme was upset through the incessant rain. One item of interest—nine girls were presented with Lower Primary Certificates for the first time in the history of the school (which is only a few years old of course), so there was great excitement over that and much clapping of hands and general enthusiasm. Later on a bran-pie for [a 100] outside Sunday School children caused a good deal of fun. Chinese tea and all sorts of wonderful cakes were handed round to everyone . . . About 5 p.m. we had to move over to the Women's School and dress the tree for the 'grown-ups' . . . illuminated with dozens of little candles, which was a wonderful sight to some of the old ladies who have come into the Station class as 'inquirers', and had never seen anything like it. I remember one dear old lady over 70 saying in rapt admiration, 'Can Heaven be more beautiful than this?' or something to that effect. It is a relief to have Christmas happily over once more; it is a most strenuous time out in the Mission field, but delightfully happy time all the same—the joy and privilege of bringing 'joy, bright joy' to so many lives that are lived so much 'in the shade, until 'the light of the glorious Gospel of Christ' has shone into their hearts . . . I have much enjoyed having the Women's School this term, and feel someone has been praying for us. We have had such a bright, peaceful term, thank God! I have had 29 dear women under my care this quarter—all of them so sweet one does so long that every one may be 'bright gems in his crown in that day when he makes up his jewels.' Our schools close in about ten days' time, January 21st, so all are reading hard for their exams, which begin in a day or two. When school is over

I hope to get round the district, itinerating as much as possible before we re-open again at the beginning of March.[9]

Minna's letter made Sophie keen to get back to Lieng Kong as soon as she could. But, as she needed more time to renew her strength, the local CMS Committee did not deem it time to do this till later in the year. Its Instructions reveal both a clear sense of the precarious period through which the world was living and the strenuous time she had experienced during her last term of service.

> We cannot but feel that the sending forth of three missionaries at this time in the history of our Empire through the liberality of members of the Church Missionary Association speaks eloquently of the faith of God's people in the things that matter and their firm grip on 'the things that cannot be shaken'. In these days, no one ought be surer than the missionary that they are in the very place in the world where God wants them to be. The very terror of such passions as are now rampant in Europe will drive the missionary to their God-given work with a more cogent sense that only in the deep acceptance of Gospel truth can rescue from such a world plague be found.
>
> One of you we are beginning to regard as something of a veteran in the foreign field. It is now 8 years since we first had the pleasure of sending you forth in humble dependence upon the God who has never forsaken you. Your presence here tonight as you gladly turn your face again to China is an assurance to the others that they too will never regret the step they are taking now. We are thankful to know that for a time at least that you will be taking up a work that will prove a lesser strain on your physical powers than the work at Lieng Kong. We would beg of you as of the others to do all in your power to conserve your strength. The Promise of our God is 'As thy days so shall thy strength be,' but He has never promised the strength to do two days work in one. The missionary who breaks down in the field is not only useless for service, but lays a burden upon the fellow labourers and a deep anxiety upon the home Committee, which sometimes, with care, might be avoided. We are thankful to have had you home with us again, and to have heard from your lips something of what God is doing through you and we assure you that not only the Parish of St Luke's Burwood which you represent, but the

---

9. Reported later in the *Gippsland Times*, 17 May 1915, 4.

members of the Association generally, will consistently bear you up to the Throne of Grace.[10]

When Sophie returned to China, she was appointed to replace Eugenie Little, Matron of the CMS Guest Home in Foochow, who was on furlough. Her responsibility at "The Firs" was to act as hostess to new missionaries undertaking language study, as she had done almost twenty years earlier, as well as to missionaries who needed a time of rest in the capital. This was a less demanding role than her previous one of heading up a mission station engaged in a variety of challenging ministries.

The Blind Boys School Band in uniform

During this time, Sophie was able to see Amy, her colleague from earlier Deng-doi days, and visit her Blind Boys School in the Old City. The number of students, the range of their craftwork business activities, and the opportunities the Blind Boys Band had to play at civic and public in and beyond the province, had all expanded. On 20 April, Sophie celebrated at a distance the marriage in Sydney of her sister Grace to a widower friend of the family. Never far from her thoughts, however, were seven members of her wider family who had enlisted in the Australian forces serving on the Western Front. Unfortunately, while in Foochow she caught typhoid fever again and was admitted for a month in Tak-ding Hospital in Foochow, followed by a short time of recovery in a guest room at Amy's Blind School.

---

10. "Instructions to S. S. Newton," CMA NSW, 10 January, 1915.

When Sophie returned to Lieng Kong, it was not long before the summer break. During this, some unexpected opportunities and challenges arose:

> Life here is by no means monotonous. We never know what is going to happen next. One exceptionally hot day in July, just as we were preparing to go away to the cool of the hills, we heard that one of the school girls, living nearby, had been suddenly engaged by her widowed mother as second wife to a heathen. We were very indignant about it and determined to do our utmost to prevent the marriage, but, as bracelets had been given and a feast partaken of, it seemed a most unlikely thing, from a Chinese point of view, that the engagement could be broken off.
>
> However we prayed constantly and earnestly about it, and our Chinese workers did all they could, taking journeys to and fro in the heat between the girl's house and that of the man's mother. We remonstrated with the girl's mother and tried to comfort the girl, who was most unwilling for the engagement but had been goaded to acquiescence, and was too filial to protest much. Finally we had the satisfaction of hearing that the man was willing to accept another (a heathen) girl, and the money paid by him was refunded, bracelets returned and an agreement signed, so we were able to go away with light heart.
>
> Another excitement was a flood on the very day we were to have begun the new term of the school. We watched the water rising higher and higher, but were so thankful it was no worse and no damage was done to our compound, though the people lost a great part of their crops. The girls managed to get there gradually, and now we are in full swing with 70 scholars, big and small in the Girls School.[11]

The gradual breakdown in the country after Emperor Yuan Shi-kei's death a year earlier led to growing unrest in some areas of the country. Though this did not happen in their district, at times they were affected by troop movements through it. As Sophie wrote:

> Since our return from the hills we have lived through some exciting times in connection with the coming of soldiers from the Southern Government. This time, as [Nellie] Marshall has been borrowed by another hospital, our medical work is in the temporary charge of the Chinese pastor's daughter.

---

11. S. S. Newton, "Jottings from Lieng Kong", *Diocese of Fukien Magazine*, 1917, 15–16.

One day when soldiers were pouring in from Foochow, she came to consult us about going to a case in a village about eight miles away, in the direction from which the soldiers were coming. As the man who had come to ask her to go said his daughter-in-law was seriously ill, and seemed most urgent in his request, we agreed that she might go with an escort (the man himself, our watchman and a Chinese nurse).

It was nearly dark when they finally set out. They met soldiers all along the narrow road who were not very polite and tried to push the chairs aside to get them out of the way, so they soon came back and agreed to start next morning. This they did but had not got very far when they met a messenger to say the woman had died, and the family blamed the soldiers for the delay.[12]

Along with resuming work in both the Girls and Womens Schools, Sophie sought opportunities to balance these with occasional trips to distant villages. She was able to do this partly because Huang Ong, the first girl whose education had been supported by her cousin and other Christians in Nowra, had graduated from the Teachers Training College in Foochow and returned as a teacher in the Girls School.

Regarding her trips to remote parts of the District, Sophie wrote:

> When we can manage to get away for weekend visits to country churches they are always appreciated by the Christians, especially in places where there is no catechist or Bible woman. To those who are accustomed to the beautiful old churches in some of our villages at home, where the very atmosphere seems conducive to reverence and quiet, these village churches are painfully noisy and un-church-like. In some cases it is the 'common' room of a family or families that is used for worship on Sundays, the things in everyday use being cleared away and a few forms set out for the purpose, a table and two chairs at the top serving as a chancel.
>
> If the house is shared by a heathen they may come in and out during the service, making remarks in their ordinary loud voices. In any case, small children and the household animals prove disturbing elements. Two of our village congregations 'made do' with such rooms up till now, but the number of Christians has increased, and accommodation has become quite inadequate.[13]

---

12. S. S. Newton, "Jottings from Lieng Kong", *Diocese of Fukien Magazine*, 1917, 16–17.

13. S. S. Newton, "Jottings from Lieng Kong", *Diocese of Fukien Magazine*, 1917, 17–18.

The following month, Sophie began to experience symptoms that could stem from typhoid. This was confirmed by a visit to the CMS doctor in Foochow. In early October he gave her a Medical Certificate approving "leave on grounds of health in order to proceed to Australia and that such a change is absolutely necessary for restoration of health."[14] On 9 November, after little more than a year back in the field, Sophie left for Foochow and then by boat to Hong Kong. Five days later she boarded a Japanese steamer, *SS Aki Marei*, arriving in Sydney ten days before Christmas.

Over the next eighteen months, Sophie continued to speak to churches and Christian groups about China, mostly about the state of women there. These focussed on the continuing practice of betrothals of young girls, the large decline of infanticide, and the dying out of foot-binding. She also spoke about the way girls' education resulted in less hierarchical forms of marriages, wives taking up part-time work alongside family responsibilities and, in some cases, their training as bible-women, nurses, teachers, and occasionally doctors.[15] Occasionally Sophie also enjoyed having a conversation in Chinese with someone from China, surprising them by falling easily and fluently into their dialect when it transpired that they came, as many did, from Fukien.[16]

At this time, Sophie wrestled with three potential obstacles to resuming her work in China. One was passing the retirement age for women of fifty-five before her next term of service finished, as it was unsure whether CMS would approve her return. Another consideration was her periodic tendency to illness. A third was her mother's advancing age and, since her daughter Grace's marriage, living on her own. What the Committee would decide about the first two matters was uncertain, but her mother and closest sisters encouraged her to return to China. In February, to her delight, the CMS Committee approved a further term of service and, through her practice of "waiting on God," God gave her a promise that her mother could be left in His care. A few weeks later, the family members in Sydney held a day of "extended time of prayer" to ask God's help and wisdom for each of them until they could all be together again.

On 29 March 1918, Sophie boarded the *SS Aki Maru* again, this time sailing via Manila, and reached Foochow on 5 May. While she was away, a

---

14. Fukien Precis Book, 24 November 1916.

15. *The Sun*, 10 December, 1916, 14, reproduced in the *Barrier Miner*, 23 December 1916, 7.

16. *The North Western Gazette*, 7 March, 1916, 2.

new bishop had been appointed who was to play an important part in her life. John Hind was from Belfast and a graduate of Trinity College, Dublin. Aged only thirty-nine, he had already served in Fukien for sixteen years, the last seven as Principal of the Anglican Boys School and then President of Trinity Theological College. Sophie was fascinated to discover what she felt was a providential link between the two of them. The very person who had started the deaconess order in Sydney, Rev Mervyn Archdall, now a Bishop in Ireland, had ordained John Hind to work in China.[17]

Bishop John Hind

Since Sophie was arriving mid-way through the last term of the academic year, there was little sense in her going to Lieng Kong. Instead, she was deputized to take over a part of Miss Little's responsibility at "The Firs," that of supervising the work of Day Schools on Nantai as she had done two years earlier. This appealed to her "country girl" origins. Since it involved walking for one or two hours between each the five schools scattered around the island, it brought back memories of her early years wandering around the districts where she was raised. It also reminded her of her time as a governess to children in the outback. While, during this time, she felt that "life

---

17. The bishop wrote a brief memoir of his time in China: Hind, *Fukien Memories*.

is full of happy and useful service to my fellow-workers, both foreign and Chinese,"[18] her headaches began to return, resulting in a month's stay at Tak-Ding Hospital. The stress of wondering whether she and her mother "may not see each other on earth again", and wondering whether she "ought to be well and at work" in more significant ways, were no doubt factors in this condition recurring.[19] Sophie obviously found it difficult to view this more relaxed time God's gift toward restoring her to full health.

In November 1918, she returned to her old district. On the way, a thief broke into the boat and stole a number of her most personal possessions. As some of these had been given to her by her family, she found this quite distressing. When she arrived at the mission compound, another loss was finding that as her previous responsibilities had been taken over by others, she was now designated to undertake temporary duties, or "piece-work"[20] as she called it, assisting others in different aspects of their work. In her absence, Hung Ong had returned from the Teacher Training College in Foochow to teach in the Girls School. This was a significant development in local education. Much to Sophie's delight, Ai-cio would soon be joining her. In the school, there was more consistent attendance, a higher rate of retention, and a stronger ambition among many girls for a different way of life to their elders. Some had gone on to become Sunday School teachers, and a few were training to become teachers in day schools.

Everything in the mission complex paused briefly on 11 November to celebrate the end of the Great War. Sophie gave thanks for members of her family who had survived the slaughter. Among her relatives, several of whom she had taught in Warialda, two were awarded the Military Cross, three were wounded, and three had sadly been killed. Though, as a nation, China was not officially involved in the War, through its voluntary Chinese Labour Corps, thousands of its citizens had worked tirelessly behind the lines as support workers along the Western Front.[21]

On the wider front, flowing from her long-standing interest in the Jewish people, Sophie became secretary for the international Prayer Union for Israel and editor of its quarterly newsletter.[22] Her involvement

18. S. S. Newton, Annual Letter, February 1920, 2.
19. Citing entries for this part of 1918 in her Fourth Journal.
20. See S. S. Newton, Annual Letter, 28 November, 1.
21. O'Neill, *Chinese Labour Corps*.
22. The Prayer Union for Israel dated back to 1880 and it was through George Grubb that it was fused with the Christian Mission to the Jews.

in this movement stemmed as far back as her call to the mission field, when George Grubb had talked passionately about the needs of God's covenant. In Fukien, Bishop Hind's official endorsement of this ministry was a great encouragement.

Since the Nationalist government had come to power for nearly a decade, life for people in the district had gradually improved. However, the decrease in political unity resulted in more groups of brigands roaming the countryside, even in parts of Lieng Kong. On occasions, this hindered the missionaries' freedom to move around the villages. At this time, several natural disasters also affected the district. A severe outbreak of cholera resulted in many deaths, and a powerful typhoon, followed by a tsunami higher than anyone could remember, caused widespread damage and further loss of life. In the mission compound, the water saturated fifty rooms, which took workmen three months to clean and repair.

While Sophie was at Kuliang in the summer of 1919, significant changes were made to the way mission work was conducted in Fukien. Bishop Hind was committed to loosening Western control of the nearly three hundred churches in the province and giving greater control to the Chinese nationals. He insisted that nationals preside at all meetings, the Chinese language alone be spoken at all diocesan meetings, and bible-women be given an official place in church structures. In Hind's words, these changes were all designed to make "the Chinese Christians feel that the church was their own, and also to remove from the minds of non-Christians the idea that the Christian church was a foreign organisation."[23] Sophie was strongly supportive of all these progressive reforms.

At the Kuliang Summer Conference, the CMS Womens Sub-Committee decided that the following year Sophie look after the innovative Girls Middle School in Foochow whole its Principal was away on furlough. Disappointed that this was another temporary appointment, she drew strength from the biblical injunction to "humble yourselves before the Lord, and he will lift you up" (James 4:10). In her journal during this period, she talks several times about how she had come to understand that obedience to God eventually results in a quietness of spirit in the midst of everyday activities, and that acceptance of His will brings greater flexibility in difficult situations and consideration of other's needs.

On the personal front at this time, Sophie was delighted by Daik-Hok's delayed graduation from teacher training in Foochow. During his time in

---

23. John Hind, Letter to the Review Diocesan Committee, 21 October 1921.

the army and afterwards, he had kept her words about keeping love of God first in his life, and was coming back to the Lieng Kong district to teach in a mission school in the district. Meanwhile Ai-cio, who was now teaching in the Girls School, had fallen in love with the local pastor's third son.

> He fell in love with her and asked his father to secure *her* for him (true Eastern fashion!). The pastor asked my permission as I was her Guardian. I said she must wait till she was eighteen, a rule of the church.[24]

When that time came, Sophie had the pleasure making all arrangements about the trousseau and other aspects of the wedding as well as of giving the bride away. As she was no longer Ai-co's guardian, she also felt free to accept a similar responsibility for a young boy and his sister whose parents could no longer take care of them and no relatives were in a position to do so.

During her final months in Lieng Kong, Sophie made a round of visits to nearby villages. In a few places, she conducted a week-long mission, preaching primarily to women, but sometimes a small number of men as well. So encouraging were the results that she wished she had done this before. On one of these trips, she fell over the edge of a steep embankment, but was fortunately rescued by her porters and escaped with only minor injuries. Sophie also made a last visit to the house in Deng-doi where the "little band of sisters" had lived many years ago. As it was no longer needed for a missionary team, CMS had decided to sell it. She walked again up the hill behind the house to look across at the faraway pagoda where the original band of women had envisioned their work.

> Within twenty years what strides have been made in Lieng Kong! No ladies were living there, only two or three were visiting, but on 1 January 1898, we moved into the new house at Deng-doi, and then the work went ahead.
>
> We held Sunday school for the women in the morning, and for the children in the afternoon, First a very few, a mere handful, and oh! how [we] the teachers stumbled, how little they could say, but they said they could, and now that Sunday school is the largest and most flourishing in the district, and chiefly managed by one of the first Chinese scholars.
>
> No woman could read then: now hundreds have passed through the women's school and can read well. Then only two or

---

24. S. S. Newton, "Letter to Supporters in Nowra."

three women had unbound their feet; now hundreds have done so, as well as refraining from binding their children's feet.

Then no hospital: now a nice little one. Then no girls boarding school; now a large one, always full. And what about itinerating work? Then it was very difficult to get a clean and comfortable place to stay in: now we have many centres where we may stay for days, or even weeks, either to visit distant villages or to hold classes for the women.[25]

---

25. This is drawn from a summary she had written a little earlier under the title "What Has Happened in Two Decades?", *CMS Home Gazette*, July 1917, 165.

# 6

Recalled to Wider Service in the City of Banyan Trees

AT THE START OF the new school year in September 1919, Sophie packed up her things and moved to Foochow. After the boat docked at the wharf on Nantai Island, she hired a rickshaw to take her to the CMS House. Her route took her through familiar streets bordered by ancient banyan trees, the symbol of the city and over a thousand in number. Passing these trees, she reflected on how far she had come since she spent time there as a new missionary studying the language. Sophie saw the trees, whose branches not only reached out but appeared to go down into the ground, as a parable of how far she had matured and how deep her roots now reached into her adopted homeland. As the trees grew very slowly from little seeds and, when full-grown, were renowned for the amount of shade they gave, they also mirrored the gradual progress of the gospel in China and the refuge it provided from corrosive elements in the wider culture. Since banyans were a variety of fig trees, for her there were biblical associations as well.

CMS Girls School on Nantai Island

The Girls Middle School where she was Acting-Principal was the only one of its kind in Fukien Province. It provided advanced studies for girls to prepare them for the widening range of work opportunities now opening up. At the time there were around two hundred and fifty girls in the school. Together with the assistant principal, Dorothy Stubbs, Sophie oversaw the school, worked with staff and parents, and undertook a little teaching. As well as a new spirit of patriotism among the girls, she noticed more willingness to ask questions and engage in discussion rather than, as in the past, largely listen and absorb. Teaching them the Bible, she observed, since they entered into its world so quickly and saw things she missed, brought home how much it was an Eastern book.

Sophie also found parents had a greater desire to invest in their daughters' education. This change of attitude showed the extent of the "educational as well as social revolution" of it instigated by the work of female missionaries like Sophie. When some of these students progressed to the Normal School and Women's College in Foochow, many girls from poorer as well as wealthier homes began to critically examine Chinese traditions concerning women and family. They began to demand equal treatment with their brothers and eventually moved into the professions of teaching, medicine, and Christian ministry.

Sophie's study at the CMS Girls School

A special occurrence one Sunday during this time at the school was being asked to assist the bishop with services when his chaplain was ill. This was a reminder of working as a deaconess in Sydney and that she missed certain aspects of that responsibility. The most important event in the mid-1920s was an official recognition of her good friend Amy Oxley Wilkinson. In view of her twenty-year service in the Blind School, first in Deng-doi, then in Foochow, the city's literati and elders had taken the unusual step of petitioning the President in Peking to grant her a special award. "The Order of the Golden Grain" was the most distinguished honor that could be conferred on a foreigner in China, and had only been granted once before. Hau Shi-chang had consented to this and a special day was set aside in early July for the event. This began with a public procession through the city accompanied by the Governor's band, after which a celebration was held in the grounds of the Blind School.

> On the way to her house flags were flying all down the main streets in her honor. The big gate to the house was festooned with a thick arch of evergreen and flowers. A great platform had been erected in the garden with a large white awning over it to keep out the sun. On the bottom of the lawn were seats for the Chinese ladies. The foreigners sat on the terraces. There were about 1000 people present. All the rooms in the house were prepared—the drawing room for the officials, the dining room for the less important men

and the study for the ladies. Out in the garden under the trees, a grand lunch was prepared.[1]

Among the dignitaries were the Governor-General, City Mayor, and Chairman of the Chamber of Commerce. After the presentation of Honorary Boards by three Confucian and several Educational bodies, the program included the little Blind Girls' School drill, the Blind Boys' School Kindergarten, the Chinese and British National Anthem, the Blind Boys School Choir, the British National Anthem, the Presentation of Medals, commendatory speeches in Chinese and English, and Amy's reply, given in English but translated into Mandarin. The event concluded with an elaborate and lengthy afternoon tea.

From mid-July to late August, Sophie and a missionary friend spent time at Kuliang. They lived in one of the stone residences on the side of a hill. During this visit, Sophie put together a special sixteen-page booklet with photos to send to her nieces and nephews in Australia. As well as containing interesting details of daily life at this summer location, it reveals some of Sophie's skills and creativity as a teacher of young children.

> My dear Twenty-Two,
>
> This is to be a circular letter for Christmas and so I am beginning it in good time here so it will greet you all beforehand. This year, as usual, I went up to Kuliang during the great heat of July and August. We have a very busy time, though it is really supposed to be a rest. We had our Conference and all kinds of other meetings about the work and I often sit for five hours a day, which is very tiring. But it is nice and cool and the change generally does one good. This year I shared a house with Miss Matthews from Ryde. It is the opposite side of the mountain to where I usually stay at 'Waratah' (which always reminds me of Australia), so I was saved the steep climb up the hill for which I was thankful.
>
> I hope you will be interested in the pictures in this booklet. Miss Matthews has a camera and the Amah (Chinese helper) took the pictures of both of us. The first is of the house we stayed in and you can see it up the top through the trees: the foreground is the next door house with a bank between us where a Jewish lady and her husband live. I have learned a great deal about Jewish people

---

1. This is drawn from an account by a missionary, Edith Norton, contained in Ian Welch, *Letters of Amy Oxley*, a three-page item (unnumbered) preceding Appendix 1. Another account may be found in the *Church Missionary Society Gleaner*, 1 November 1920, 245.

from her. Our house has four rooms and we are very sheltered from typhoons, though the house suffered badly last year. It was built by the French Consul for his family and evidently, judging by the small furniture, there were two tiny children—but sad to say the white furniture looks so nice to the white ants too!

My next picture shows us having our breakfast under the banjo awning in front of the house. It gives you an idea of the view we enjoyed while having our meals. It was too hot in the middle of the day to have our dinner, but we enjoyed morning and evening.

Breakfast on the verandah in Kuliang

Can you recognise The Sydney Morning Herald? And the white mosquito net cover over the butter? We have to protect our food from flies out here so much because of epidemics of cholera and these wire frames covered with net are most useful because they can be boiled!

Here is a picture of Miss Matthews who is in charge of the Blind Boys School while Mrs Wilkinson is on furlough. She loves the boys and is getting on well with all of them. Can you see my little Kitty? The black spot on the cameras is a small puppy who insisted on staying with us. We have named him Chang. He is very mischievous and after the photograph was taken ran away for six days!

Missionary outing on way to the Moon Temple

The next day we had breakfast by the Moon Temple, about one and a half hours walk from Kuliang proper—such a lovely spot. We had a good climb and as usual missed the road because there are so many tracks one rarely goes direct!

Here is my bedroom and the study now at the CMS Girls School. I am writing this at the table. Some of you may recognise the green cloth with the fringe—Albert, Laurie and Ray on the mantelpiece and Hilda as a tiny girl can be seen. Grandma and Auntie Grace are on the wall—and the others scattered about. When I get homesick and want to see you, I get my little blue box in which I have put you all and just sit down and have a good look, pray for you and look forward someday to seeing you once more. On the study wall in front of me is a picture of St Luke's Burwood with the four daughter churches around her.

Now I do hope that you will not be very tired looking at all these pictures of your old Auntie in China—in a novel Christmas Card. I've decided to ask Aunt Amy to take charge of it, then I shall know it reaches you all. Who will write or send a message to their faraway Auntie saying how you like it—and anything else you want to say? I send you all my dearest love and may God bless you,

Your loving old,

Auntie in China.

Later that year, Sophie took part in the annual Christmas procession that was one of the main opportunities for public Christian witness in Foochow. This event always attracted a lot of attention in Chinese and English newspapers. As the procession passed a Christian's house or a church, firecrackers announced the fact. Leaflets about Christianity were also distributed to the crowds looking on. Unhappily for Sophie, she came down with influenza and ended up again in Tak-ding Hospital.

After Clara Lambert returned, Sophie was asked to take charge of the CE[ZM]S School on Nantai Island while its Principal was on furlough. She enjoyed the close interaction with mainly non-Christian students, and was deeply moved when some "profess to believe, and really show proofs of and are willing to take a stand for Christ, but it means much testing and trial for there are many home difficulties to contend with. Numbers of them have so refined and well-to-do and have been accustomed to the best of everything. I shall never forget the numberless private talks I had with them in my study when they told me about their trials and difficulties in the holidays and their efforts to be true, to pray, and read the bible when all in the world were opposed."[2] She was impressed by the way the girls supported anything good taking place in the school, and appointed a bible-woman to develop closer links with parents who were not believers. Though her assignment at the school felt like filling in for someone else, such experiences gave her a stronger sense that it was "the place of God's choice."

During the autumn term, Sophie inadvertently ate some contaminated meat and became very ill, at one point even fearing she might not survive. This was not an uncommon experience for missionaries in China, and it was one of the occasional everyday risks involved in living there. Despite this, a key contribution she was able to make during this period was overseeing the move of the government-run Foochow Normal School to the same campus as the Girls' School. Though she could not know it, this was a preliminary step in the formation of Fuzhou Normal University many years later.

梁劉柔芬

At the beginning of 1922, Sophie celebrated the twenty-fifth anniversary of her arrival in China. As it happened, her desktop calendar reading the day before was from Psalm 37:4, the passage God had given her when

---

2. S. S. Newton, Annual Letter, 12 December 1921, 1.

she dedicated her life to his service. She was overcome with gratitude and amazement, as her journal records: "Oh the wonder of it! Utterly unworthy of such an honor and privilege."[3] It was a great encouragement when Bishop Hind invited her to become the first deaconess in the Diocese which, since she was already ordained, would only involve her installation.

Since later that year she would reach the official retirement age for CMS missionaries, Sophie requested the General Committee "for her services to be retained in the Mission while able to work satisfactorily ... where most needed."[4] The Committee eagerly approved, and it is interesting to note that the next item for discussion was Bishop Hind's desire for someone to replace the troublesome Miss Little at "The Firs."

Bishop Hind's plan to introduce deaconesses in Fukien Diocese was novel in practice rather than in principle. Deaconesses had existed for some time in Lutheran (from the 1830s), Anglican (1860s), Episcopalian (1899), and American Methodist (1894) denominations in the West. However, only a small number of Lutheran missionaries had so far come to China from Germany and Scandinavia. American Methodists were well represented, in Foochow as well as elsewhere, but two deaconesses who arrived in China from 1908 seem to have only served in hospitals rather than in any ehurch capacity. At the turn of the century, there had been four Anglican deaconesses in Peking, but they were attached to the British Legation rather than working with the Chinese. While the Lambeth Conference in England had been discussing their responsibilities until mid-century and, as early as 1918, it was agreed in Hong Kong that deaconesses might be a valuable adjunct to the work of clergy, nothing was done to implement this. Following the appointment of an Anglican deaconess in North China in 1921, Bishop Hind was the first to install one in South China.[5]

On 24 April 1922, a little over thirty years since she had become a deaconess in Sydney, Sophie become the first deaconess in the Diocese of Fukien. As she was already ordained, all that was required was a licence her this work. This took place during a small service in Bishop Hind's study, with only Archdeacon Ding Ing-ong present. The archdeacon began the ceremony by describing the basis for the office and its main responsibilities. He referred to the women who ministered to Jesus, the help Paul received

---

3. S. S. Newton, Fourth Journal, 24 April 1922.
4. CMS General Committee, Foochow, 21 April 1922.
5. Peter Cunich, "Deaconesses in the South China Mission", 94.

from Priscilla, the work of Phoebe for the church in Cenchreae, as well as the deaconesses in the churches founded by the apostles.

> Doubt not, therefore, that our Lord Jesus Christ will accept the service of all who love Him, and the desire to assist in the feeding and nurturing of His flock. Doubt not that it is according to His will, and the true order of His church, that in the Holy Order of Deaconess women should visit the sick, comfort the afflicted, supply the wants of the poor and needy, instruct and exhort the faithful, teach the ignorant, win the children, and lovingly help to bring back the wanderers to the Shepherd and Bishop of souls. To which Holy Office our sister now desires to be admitted.[6]

女执事

The word "deaconness" in Chinese

Sophie then gave an oath of allegiance to the office, after which the bishop, drawing on Paul's letters to the Corinthians, said a few words about basing her work on the solid foundation of Christ as well as the pressures and difficulties this would bring.

The Archdeacon then prayed:

> Almighty God, giver of all good things, who of thy great goodness has vouchsafed to accept this thy servant, Sophie, into the office of Deaconess in this church. Make her, we beseech Thee, O Lord, to be modest, humble and content in her ministration, and to have a ready will to observe all spiritual discipline that she, having always the testimony of a good conscience, and continuing ever stable and strong in Thy Son Jesus Christ. May she so well behave herself in that ministry that she may be numbered among those Blessed Ones whom the Lord when He cometh shall find watching. Grant this for the sake of the same Jesus Christ Thy Son, to whom with Thee and the Holy Spirit shall be ascribed all majesty and dominion now and forevermore. Amen.

---

6. The next two quotes come from the "Form and Manner for the Ordaining of Deaconesses in the Diocese of Fukien," Anglican Diocese of Fukien, 1922.

After this, Bishop Hind closed with the Benediction. In her journal, Sophie described the occasion as "perhaps the most apparently important event to me, and indirectly to the work among women in our Mission."[7] She knew that, for the bishop, it was a first step towards ordaining other missionaries and ultimately Chinese bible-women as deaconesses. She longed for that day this would happen, as it would broaden the ministry of women throughout the province in significant ways.

A little over a month later, the archdeacon gave Sophie a public opportunity to act in her new role. Initially, she hesitated:

> I felt it was not necessary in places where there were plenty of clergy in Foochow, but when he said he felt it was a good thing to let the Christians see what office a Deaconess is entitled to perform, I felt I dare not refuse him. And so it came to pass that after preaching at the morning service, I, an English Deaconess, assisted a Chinese Archdeacon to baptise eight women and girls, and five infants, on that Sunday 4 June 1922.[8]

She was grateful that the archdeacon conducted the baptisms, as sometimes babies cried and resisted! He then asked Sophie to read the service and preach the sermon on a monthly basis in the chapel of the Girls Middle School. So successful was Sophie's acceptance by the wider church into this role, that just a few months later on 13 September, Bishop Hind felt confident to ordain six more women missionaries to the work of deaconess in the diocese.

As time went on, deaconesses increasingly served alongside Chinese pastors in churches throughout Fukien Province. They were expected to function just like deacons—as substitutes for the pastors in conducting weddings, funerals, baptisms of women and girls, leading services, and preaching. They fulfilled so much of the pastor's role that when they visited widely scattered out-stations, believers who had come from a long distance were frequently disappointed to discover that they could not celebrate Holy Communion.

梁劉柔芬

In the last week of July 1922, Sophie sought relief from the summer heat on the picturesque island of Sharp Peak rather than at Kuliang. Here there was

7. S. S. Newton, Fourth Journal, 24 April 1922.
8. S. S. Newton, Annual Letter, December 1922, 2–3

only a small fishing village, three sanatoriums, and two mission guesthouses. She enjoyed walking on the beach, which was surrounded by high sand dunes, as well as along the narrow paths that curled around the hillsides. With the luxury of a suite to herself in the CMS house, she was able to catch her breath after the busyness of the previous months and reflect on where her work as a deaconess might take her. On 26 July, she received an answer in the form of a letter from Bishop Hind appointing her as superintendent of "The Firs," the CMS mission house on Foochow's Nantai Island.

The background to this may now be filled out more fully. Towards the end of the previous year, the bishop had written a confidential memo explaining the problems at "The Firs."

> I am very sorry to have to turn to a very unpleasant subject, and one which it is not easy to speak about. I have felt for some time that it was a matter that would have to be tackled sooner or later . . . and it is time to ask for your advice and help. 'The Firs', as you know, is the CMS up-country house for women workers, and is under the charge of Miss L[ittle] as things are now, no missionary goes to the place if she can avoid it, or for no longer than she can help. One trembles at the thought of new missionaries gaining their first impressions of missionary life in that house. The conversation is anything but helpful . . . Women's Conference dare not recommend that any of the new lady missionaries should attend the Language School because it means that they must stay at 'The Firs'. I do not want you to misunderstand. My own relations with Miss L. are perfectly happy and I know her to be well meaning and sincerely interested in the whole work of the mission, but there is a kind of sneering criticism in most of her conversation, and an unkindly harshness towards most of her fellow-missionaries which is quite harmful, and is I believe a source of real danger . . . She has been spoken to many times but with little result. She takes offence easily and one only fears that a well-meant effort to try to help her may make things harder. Her furlough is nearly due but I hear that she is not proposing to take it. It has not been an easy task to write this and I hope I have not failed in either truth or charity.[9]

Soon after, the Bishop asked Sophie if she would be willing to take on this responsibility if Miss Little could be induced to resign. Though she wondered whether this was another case of "filling a gap," friends pointed out that it was a wonderful affirmation by the bishop of her capabilities.

---

9. John Hind, Letter to the Diocesan Review Committee, 21 October, 1921.

"The Firs" was, after all, the pastoral introduction in the Mission for all new women missionaries and the pastoral refuge for all existing ones in need of recuperation. Since, conveniently, "The Firs" was next door to the Bishop's House, it would enable her to have regular contact and fellowship with him.[10] Since it was also close to the Theological College, where committees and synods frequently met, there would be opportunities for ministry to a wider range of people.

Her first challenge, however, was dealing with the aging, and rather angular, Miss Little, whose furlough did not begin until later in the year. On her first day in her new position, Sophie wrote:

> Here I am in permanent charge of 'The Firs'. My first Sunday. I cannot realise it until Miss Little returns and vacates: it will not be the same. I have been meditating on James 1:5 and need desperately 'the wisdom which issues from above'.[11]

However, the day after Miss Little arrived on 10 October, Sophie was confronted with a much greater challenge, a military conflict on Foochow's doorstep. A general background to this contained two elements. Weak central government continued to result in provincial governors or warlords and their personal armies fighting over much of the country. During the 1920s, a succession of such military leaders initiated several hundreds of smaller or larger wars. Some of these conflicts involved a few hundred men on each side, while others involved up to a million troops with all the modern weapons of war—tanks, armored trains, gunboats, and aircraft. In these battles, millions of civilians, and hundreds of thousand soldiers, lost their lives. Though Fukien largely escaped these conflicts, the northern part of the province, around cities like Fu'an, was sometimes caught up in one.

Within this general framework, in south China Sun Yat-sen had sought to establish a national republican army. In the north, supported by warlords seeking to advance their regional interests, a northern army sought to defend the status quo. In late 1922, troops loyal to Sun-Yat-sen came down the Min River to expel unwelcome northern forces that were presently occupying it. The provincial government in Foochow supported the southern forces, and was dismayed when most of its schools were disbanded and taken over by troops from the north. While mission and church schools

---

10. This detail is not clear in reports before the *Fukien News*, November 41, 67.
11. S. S. Newton, Fourth Journal, 27 August 1922.

were left to carry on without interruption, protests organized by radical students at Trinity Theological College led to its closure.[12]

Over the next three days, there was fierce fighting outside the city's West and North Gates, and a gunboat guarded the Bridge of Ten Thousand Ages to prevent Northern troops retreating to Nantai Island. As the CMS compound was just over the bridge, it was vulnerable to gunfire from the battle. The fighting continued for a further week, and during this time many soldiers from the Northern Army laid down their weapons or joined the Southern troops. "In the Old City," wrote Bishop Hind, "practically all of our buildings were hit by bullets and the roofs pierced, but our workers carried on cheerfully."[13] To avoid looting by the troops, large numbers of people packed up their possessions and headed off to the foreign settlements on Nantai or to outlying villages. For five days there was an unbroken stream of men, women, and children crossing over the bridge to the island. Nantai was filled with refugees, and all available accommodation, including "The Firs," sought ways to house some of the refugees.

After the excitement died down, Sophie still had to handle the challenge of dealing with Miss Little. Over the next two months, she refers again and again in her journal to God's promise to his servants who experience 'a thorn in the flesh,' as "My grace is sufficient for you, for my power is made perfect in weakness" (2 Corinthians 12:9). These entries probably refer to Miss Little. keeping her busy with trivial demands. A working trip to the district of Lieng Kong gave Sophie some respite, and she was relieved when Miss Little left on her final furlough in December. She saw her work at "The Firs" primarily in terms of being that of a servant. She set out to make the house a "home" for newly arrived lady missionaries as they started to learn the language; a "safe" place to talk about their placements and strategies for beginning their ministry; a place of "rest" and "counsel" for visitors from inland stations or those convalescing from illness, a "base" for purchasing items that up-country missionaries required for their work; and a "center" for occasional committees, synods, and other meetings.

Since looking after "The Firs" still brought with it responsibility for supervising the Day Schools on Nantai, Sophie arranged a tour around the island. Though the number of schools had increased, these were facing two new challenges.

---

12. On the wider political developments and conflicts during this period, see Hsiu, *Rise of Modern China*, 514–34.

13. John Hind, Letter to Dr Williams, 22 October 1922.

This year we have to take into account the unsettled state of the province for it interfered a good deal with the regular attendance of the pupils, added to this there were the usual hindrances to those who are able to work. In one School all the second-year scholars and many of the First Year go to sort tea, and are away for four months at least. They are able to earn quite a good sum of money according to their ability and speed. In one village even the schoolroom has to be given up, this is included in the terms for renting the house. All this is very discouraging for the teachers. But, on consideration, one still feels these Day Schools are a great help and we must do our best with what we can get till compulsory education is introduced.[14]

On weekends, Sophie continued to assist Bishop Hind and Archdeacon Ding at church services in Foochow and nearby districts. Every so often, as part of assisting missionaries, she had to make contact with the wider foreign community, including the British Consul and Chinese leaders in the city. In the summer months, when missionaries were out of the city, oversight of a sister house to "The Firs" in Kuliang.

The following year, two personal events strongly affected her. First was the marriage of Daik-hok in Lieng Kong. Later that year, the young couple had their first child, a daughter, who they named Maorong. Sophie now had her first "grand-daughter." Second, was hearing from home that her mother was becoming more frail. As Sophie prayed through the news and talked this over with the bishop, he reminded her that if she went on furlough, CMS NSW may not let her return because she was nearing retirement age. Sophie's frustration about the situation was exacerbated by the knowledge that there was still unfinished work for her in China. Did God really want her to go back now? In the meantime, she represented the diocese at a meeting in Shanghai for leading missionaries from all over the country. This meeting brought her into contact with two people, Bishop Howard and Dorothy Mowll, who were to play a major part in her later life.

As time passed and more anxious correspondence came from home, Sophie decided to visit Lieng Kong in her January break. While there, she managed to catch up with her adoptive family, visit twelve churches and spend time at Deng-doi where she found everything going well. After returning to Foochow, she packed up all her belongings for the first time since she had come to China and made her farewells around the city. The day of her departure came all too soon. Passing under the umbrella of

14. Fukien Original Papers, 1923.

the banyan trees, which were vibrant with life now that it was spring, the rickshaw reached the dock where the boat awaited her. In Hong Kong, she was welcomed in the Christian community not just as a fellow CMS missionary but as an Anglican deaconess. She also had opportunity to link up with a member of the Stewart family, Mildred, and her husband Reg, who she had not met before. This was timely, as they were also going back to their home country uncertain as to whether a return to China was possible. After this, Sophie boarded the SS *Arafura*, arriving in Sydney towards the end of April 1924.

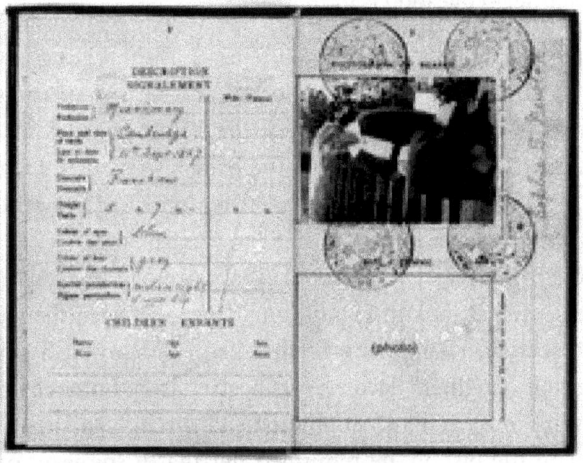

A copy of Sophie's passport

After her return to Australia, Sophie felt more unsettled than she had ever felt before. How could she best care for her mother and connect with her family after six years away? After a brief stay at "Ormskirk," her sister Amy's house in Burwood, she found herself with nowhere to go. For whatever reason, Amy's husband Harry did not want her to stay with them again. Did her way of life challenge his well-off lifestyle? Did she speak too directly at times about certain things? Did he feel Amy had been carrying the burden of care for her mother too long? We do not know. What we do know is that Sophie felt like a failure during her time at Amy's home, and she experienced a sense that "a prophet has no honor in his own city."[15]

---

15. This is a rough translation of Mark 6.4.

RECALLED TO WIDER SERVICE IN THE CITY OF BANYAN TREES

In May, Sophie's cousin Joan invited her to stay in their fine old house "Glynterion" in nearby Drummoyne. This was literally a "godsend," as it was close to her mother and could serve as a base for deputation. The next few months were secure and comfortable, but spiritually and mentally they were exhausting. She struggled with the fact that if she had not gone to "The Firs" but had come home earlier, life would have been better for her mother who was now weak and unhappy. Despite these feelings, Sophie experienced God's reassurance in an unexpected way.

> Last night I had a dream in which I was talking to a woman most earnestly, who had come to me saying she had seen my address in the paper and wanted to know what she had to do to be saved. I told her first to believe and trust. I take it to mean to be on the watch for seeking and leading them to Christ—oh that I may not miss my opportunity here at home.[16]

By August she felt that she was regaining a measure of wholeness, echoing the words of the half-healed man in the Gospels, "'I see men as trees walking" (Mark 8.24). In God's time he touched my eyes and helped me to see clearly again."[17] Then, in early September, she was heartened at receiving an official renewal from the Archbishop of Sydney of her licence to serve as a deaconess in the Diocese.[18]

In February 1925, Sophie and her mother were both admitted to Highbury Private Hospital in nearby Croydon. Sophie was diagnosed with congestion of the lung and Emma was so gravely ill with cancer that it was clear that her time was limited. On 10 May, surrounded by her family, Emma died at "Ormskirk." The burial service took place at St Thomas' Anglican Cemetery in the adjoining suburb of Enfield. Sophie was deeply thankful that she was able to spend the last year of her mother's life by her side. The final journal entry dealing with her mother's death captures the heartache she felt many months later:

> Christmas Eve 1925. Surely I have never felt so lonely! This time last year Mother was interested in all the Christmas preparations, giving me money to shop for her—but now she just seems to be looking down from Glory and saying how good it is to be there. What a rest this gives. The missing is only for oneself and not for

---

16. S. S. Newton, Fourth Journal, May 1924.
17. S. S. Newton, Fourth Journal, August 1925.
18. John C. Wright, "Authority of Deaconess Sophie Sackville Newton," 1 September, 1924.

her. It certainly is the alonest Christmas I have ever had, but it makes me realise His presence—I shed tears many times—but our Darling is safe and well off now—no wants—no pain—no tears—no cares—nothing to sadden our dear old Mother again. Praise God for all the comfort in the midst of loneliness. But in my heart there is also an ache for China. Is it His will? Is this the Enemy's work keeping me back? . . . Looking better, feeling better, why must I now stay here?[19]

19. S. S. Newton, Fourth Journal, 24 December 1925.

7

Passing on the Lantern and Honored by the People

> At the last meeting of the General Committee, a letter was received from Miss Newton, in which she stated that owing to the Doctor's report of her health, she felt she would not be able to return to China for a further term of service. The Committee received the information with sincere regret and placed on record a resolution, expressing its sympathy and deep appreciation of the services rendered by Miss Newton during the 29 years she had labored in China, and placed her on the retired list. Miss Newton has recently lost her mother, who for many years was devoted to the work of CMS. We greatly sympathize with Miss Newton in her disappointment at not going back to China, but feel sure she will be greatly used in the homeland.[1]

THIS ANNOUNCEMENT WOULD HAVE come as a shock to many Australian readers of *The Church Missionary Gleaner*. For Sophie, her unexpected retirement came as a second blow on top of the death of her mother.

Painfully aware that she now had no "home" to go back to in China and no "home" anywhere in Australia, miraculously she was gifted a block of land at Woodford in the beautiful Blue Mountains, nearly sixty miles west of Sydney. The benefactor was a Mrs Claydon (one of the Claydon clan who were strong proponents of CMS), who had supported Sophie since her time at Burwood. Woodford was a place that appealed to Sophie because

---

1. *Church Missionary Gleaner* (Australia), September 1925, 11. A similar announcement appeared in the St Luke's Burwood Parish Paper on 1 January 1926, 87–88.

it had a similar relationship to Sydney that Kuliang had to Foochow. It was rural in character, always cooler in summer, and a place to which people resorted for both their health and leisure. Sophie had the pick of five blocks and chose one that would enable her to build a house back from the road surrounded by a large flower and vegetable garden. Sophie placed a deposit on a new fibro cottage and gained a small loan from the Government Savings Bank for the remainder. Her "nest egg" provided the deposit, the proceeds of a sale of shares in Bundaberg Sugar Works purchased fifteen years earlier in her name. These shares were bought by Miss Ruby Starling (who had earlier donated funds to build St Peter's East Burwood) to give Sophie some security in retirement. God's timing in working out all these details amazed Sophie. If she had waited even a few years, these shares might have lost their value in the Great Depression.

On 3 March 1926, in a small ceremony with a few friends and the local rector, the foundation stone of the place she called "Isleham," after her birthplace in England, was laid. From a rented flat in the adjoining Woodford Academy, she watched the building grow. Three months later, on 17 June, "moving in to my God-given home" finally happened.[2] In the providence of God, 1926 was a year of significant reform in Australia's social welfare system. Changes in the Old Age Pension Act meant that Sophie was able to receive a sickness benefit for a year and, when she turned sixty, an annual income of £27.

Sophie continued to wrestle with God over what he wanted her to do next. Although she received two offers of work—one as a deaconess in the local area and the other a position in Orange, the first large township across the mountains—she realized that her priority was to regain full health and strength, and take needed uninterrupted rest. Despite these offers of ministry,

> Deep down I long to be with the Chinese: the more I think of them, the more my heart goes out in longing to return—such a homesick feeling for China. I believe that as He took me out the first time in 1897, after waiting 5 years and surmounting all the obstacles, He can do it again if this is His will.[3]

After only three months in her new house, a letter came from the church in Lieng Kong City, pleading with CMS to send Sophie back for one

---

2. S. S. Newton, "Account of the Dedication of Newton Cottage," in the Banks Family Collection.

3. S. S. Newton, Fourth Journal, 26 July 1925.

more term. They had missed her during her years in Foochow and valued the contribution she could make at this stage of their development.

梁劉柔芬

So, in the October issue of the local *Church Missionary Gleaner* it was noted that:

> At the monthly meeting for prayer held in the CMS Rooms on 30 August, opportunity was taken to say farewell to Miss Newton who is returning to China for the sixth time. The Rev. H.S. Begbie spoke of the long service which Miss Newton had given to China, and joined with her in giving thanks to God for having restored her to health and strength so as to make it possible for her to go. Miss Newton expressed the great joy it was to be going out once again. On every other occasion she had been 'sent', now the call had been 'come'![4]

In a remarkably short time, Sophie managed to find reliable tenants who would look after her house at Woodford and help pay off the remainder of her mortgage.

At the beginning of her sixtieth year, Sophie set off joyfully for four final years with her beloved Chinese. Meeting up after so long away with Daik-hok and Ai-cio, and their families, was for all of them wonderful. Sophie was especially touched by young Maorong immediately calling her "grandma." She was also delighted with her appointment to further educational work in the Lieng Kong district, alongside Marion Onyon, who was now the senior missionary, and Miss Scott, who had responsibility for the Womens School. This position connected her work as a deaconess to a particular church and district, and it added status to the church's work there. As well as being appointed again to the Church's Board of Education, she became a member of the Fukien Anglican Mission Committee, both of which met several times a year in the capital.

---

4. S. S. Newton, *Church Missionary Gleaner* (Australia), October 1926, 11.

Students at the Girls Boarding School in Lieng Kong City

She also set about creating a garden. The result, she said, was "a pretty artistic Chinese compound",[5] one that impressed even the British Consul when he visited the mission station sometime later. While her co-workers and the church in the city welcomed her back warmly, the Chinese Christian workers were less enthusiastic than formerly. Though personally a little disappointed at this change of attitude, Sophie recognized that missionaries simply had to accept this as a necessary development on the way to greater local autonomy. For her part, she especially enjoyed working with the head teacher at the Girls' Boarding School, one of their Chinese converts. She was greatly encouraged when she witnessed the fruits of the work begun in the day schools decades before. One student had become a clergyman, many church workers, several teaching in Boarding Schools, others trained Kindergarten teachers, two becoming doctors, and one girl who would like to be a deaconess.

A few days into the new year, the wider political situation began to impinge even more closely on missionary work in Lieng Kong and Foochow. During Sophie's absence, there had been a build-up of university and college student resentment against foreigners in Fukien. An anti-Christian federation that began in Shanghai in 1922 had spread to other port cities, including Foochow.[6] Following a strategy developed by the federation, the Students' Union organized a parade to arouse public attention, made speeches discrediting Christianity, distributed anti-Christian literature,

5. S. S. Newton, Annual Letter, 27 August 1927, 2.

6. The development of this movement may be found in Jeffrey Wasserman, *Student Protests in Twentieth Century China: The View from Shanghai*, Shanghai: Shanghai University Press, 1927.

and hung up posters with messages such as "Destroy Christian schools" and "Stay away from Christianity."

This situation was made all the more difficult by an increase in the activity of brigands in the wider province. Because of the potential danger posed by bandits operating in Lieng Kong district, the British Consul had already placed restrictions on travel to many of the villages. As the situation worsened, he ordered all the missionaries into Foochow. Sophie and her colleagues had only one night to pack their suitcases and head up the river.

In early January, anti-Christian forces in Foochow began a determined effort to eradicate Christianity in the city. Posters were hung throughout the city denouncing everything from the so-called "Unequal Treaties" of the previous century to the role of foreign churches as the "Heralds of Imperialism." Parents of students in mission schools received threatening letters telling them to withdraw their children or face injury. Though the authorities in the city repudiated these attacks, they did little to suppress them. A week later, on 10 January, Bishop Hind ordered the evacuation of all CMS missionaries in the province to Japan.

In the mid-1920s, China's political situation grew increasingly confused and uncertain. Some of this was due to the ongoing spread of Western ideas, especially through universities. Some students felt that important Chinese values were being threatened, while others began to criticize Western countries for not living up to the values they espoused. It was particularly students returning from study in the West who were most affected. This led to anti-Western, including anti-Christian, riots in Shanghai and then other cities, including Foochow and Lieng Kong. After Sun-Yat-sen's death in 1925, power in the Kuomintang passed to its military leader, Chiang Kai-Shek. In 1926, his forces marched from Canton to overthrow the rule of warlords in and around Peking, passing through Foochow where they engaged elements of the Northern Army.[7]

In the ensuing battle, rioters and some soldiers looted and set fire to two churches and the YMCA, and also intimidated local residents living nearby. Threats were then made against mission compounds. Further assaults on churches, some connected to missions, culminated on Saturday 16 January, but they were largely contained to the old city. These events made headline news not only in the local Chinese press but in newspapers around the world, and comparisons were drawn between "Black Saturday"

---

[7] The full story of the so-called Northern Expedition is set out in Jordan, *The Northern Expedition:* On Chiang-Kai-shek there, see Fenby, *China's Generalissimo*.

and what had happened during the Boxer Rebellion. If missionaries had not been evacuated a few days earlier, lives would have been lost. A few days later, with the support of American fighters and bombers, Chiang Kai-Shek's troops recaptured Lieng Kong City and moved through Deng-doi on their way north to secure other port cities.

For Sophie, evacuation to Japan meant that she was able to visit fellow Australian CMS missionary Kathleen Boydell, who was teaching at the Girls Boarding School in Kagoshama. At the end of February 1926, the missionaries from Fukien received permission to return. Back in Lieng Kong City, things were now comparatively quiet compared with other parts of the province. However, in March, students from Fukien Christian University captured and paraded the leading Chinese pastor of the Anglican Cathedral for three hours in front of the British and American Consulates on Nantai Island, threatening his life unless he recanted. He refused to do so and was only saved when Kuomintang marines broke up the mob. In April, all missionaries received orders from the consul to withdraw to Foochow, where they stayed for six weeks. Sophie stayed with the bishop, giving her opportunities for fellowship with him.

In the middle of May, trouble flared up again across the river in the older part of the city. Occupying soldiers, rather than the city's citizens, were responsible for the unrest. A Catholic orphanage was looted and the nuns were forced to flee. A Chinese church and pastor's house, the Anglo-Chinese school and residences, and the main hospital were all damaged. Several missionaries and Chinese co-workers lost their possessions, two female teachers were roughly treated and, when he sought to protect them, Dr Matthews, a fellow-Australian, was kicked and knifed. Fortunately, the trouble did not reach as far as Nantai, and within a few days the regular soldiers had asserted control.

In the meantime, Chinese staff workers in Lieng Kong City kept the mission station running, and its matron, with whom Sophie had worked for thirty years, wrote every day to keep her in touch with what was happening. The exemplary way this woman and the others carried out their duties convinced Sophie that in future more responsibility should be left in their hands.

Delayed by the usual summer break in the mountains, it was not until 10 September that Sophie and her colleagues returned to Lieng Kong. To their relief, everything in the compound was as they had left it. The next morning, however, someone had written on their boundary wall:

Down with Christianity,
the foreigners have returned,
no more peace in Lieng Kong.[8]

While this caused initial anxiety, the Chinese workers explained that the protest simply came from some young people strolling around and looking for something to do. This seemed to be confirmed by the fact that there were no further messages of this kind or any hint of further disturbance.[9]

梁劉柔芬

In October 1926, the wider political situation in China began to stabilize through the re-establishment in Peking of the first national government under Chiang Kai-Shek. Even so, some independent warlords retained power in some parts of the east coast and in the interior of the country.[10] The new government sought to modernise the nation, reform the monetary and banking system, and expand public education. It also introduced legislation to hand control of schools into Chinese rather than Western hands and to limit the amount of direct religious instruction. It was hoped that the latter policy would prevent religious instruction from detracting from teaching core subjects and enable more time to be devoted to classical Chinese texts.

The first of these changes was quickly implemented in Lieng Kong District, as Chinese staff had been running the Girls' Boarding School in the city for a year. A Chinese board of managers and a Chinese principal were formally appointed. These individuals were keen for Sophie to continue playing a significant role and they created a new position for her. She was invited to become the School Chaplain and head of the Scripture department. These two responsibilities were very congenial, the first because it drew on her experience as a deaconess, and the second because it recognized her expertise in teaching the Bible to both girls and women.

A short time later, an inspector from the Government Education Board addressed the pupils on the mandatory "Three Principles"—Nationalism, Democracy and Socialism—now governing all schools, and

8. S.S Newton, Annual Letter, 2 August 26, 1.

9. The general effects of the protests and disturbances in Fuzhou during this period are summed up by Dunch, *Fuzhou Protestants*, 126–27, as ultimately more positive than negative.

10. Jowett, *Armies of Warlord China*.

he checked to see if they were being implemented. While at the school he made some explicitly anti-foreign remarks, and when the local pastor criticized his "unnecessary" remarks, the inspector confessed that he only made these because he had been paid to do so. For the most part, the staff continued to teach freely and there was little change in the amount of Scripture taught. Indeed, the importance of Scripture lessons was underscored by the Chinese principal, who at the beginning of the new term gave a biblically-inspired talk to the student body.

The issue of greater Chinese control also affected the local churches. Here, too, Sophie sensed the winds of change and was convinced that missionaries should work with them rather than against them. As she wrote in her annual letter,

> I cannot shut my eyes to the fact that they are passing through a phase of independence when they would really like to take full control, and be able to do without us. I don't think they are conscious of it themselves, nor would they admit it but I'm convinced it is there, and if only we could leave them for a while so they could find out for themselves that we are only anxious to walk hand in hand with them, then they would welcome us back. But as this cannot be, we must be patient with them, and loving and tactful and be willing to be misunderstood and often 'let down and not go under. We must not 'hold aloof' but be sympathetic and let them manage everything they can with us nearby, 'at your service' . . .[11]

It is a credit to Sophie that, despite her advancing years, she adopted such a progressive approach to this issue, especially when the views of some of her fellow CMS missionaries were more negative and patronizing.

Throughout the remainder of 1927, Sophie's work in Lieng Kong continued as usual. Despite being denied permission to itinerate because a lady missionary had been taken captive in a nearby district, Sophie and her co-workers persuaded the local Magistrate to allow her to visit some of the village churches. Some problems arose in the city through newer Baptist and Adventist groups who were actively pushing more extreme views and seeking to lure Christians away from other churches. In Foochow, she attended Archdeacon Ding's installation as Assistant Bishop of the Diocese in late October and, a few days later, on 1 November, participated in the consecration of the new Christ Church Cathedral in Foochow. As Sophie recounts, this was a grand affair:

11. S. S. Newton, Annual Letter, 2 August 1926, 3.

> ... all eleven dioceses were represented by beautiful banners ... carried by members of the choir, three deaconesses, the clergy, and three bishops. The sermon was preached by Bishop Morris of Peking on the vision in Isaiah 6 in English ... as there were many visitors. This was interpreted by Dean Ling. The Cathedral was packed and it was a most reverent service. Everything went off without a hitch, and this in spite of the fact that for a few days there was a renewal of anti-foreign feeling ...[12]

The following year contained several highlights:

- In the New Year break she led several services in the local church and enjoyed playing afterwards with the younger children.
- When the first term began, Sophie held her regular Saturday afternoon prayer meeting for the school and a more general prayer meeting in the evening, followed by a hymn and coffee.
- In later February, she was present at what she called a "red-letter day," the ordination of two Chinese deaconesses by Bishop Hind in Foochow. One of these had been a teacher at the CMS Girls School during Sophie's time there.
- In April, an intensifying of bandit activity resulted in the recall of all missionaries to Foochow for six weeks but the work in Lieng Kong was effectively carried on by Chinese colleagues.
- Through the summer, severe storms led to a steep rise in river levels. Many were unable to worship in the city, so Sophie opened up her home for church services.
- A typhoon in early September led to severe flooding and landslides, and crops were washed away. Great distress was evident wherever one looked.

---

12. This appeared in the *Church Missionary Gleaner* (Australia), 1 February 1928, 4.

Deaconess Ding Sieu-Giong (second from left, back row), with her six sisters

Throughout this whole period, Sophie found herself frequently sustained by the thought of "her peaceful little cottage" in the Blue Mountains.

梁劉柔芬

Following these events, Sophie experienced an unexpected change in her responsibilities. She was seconded to work in Fu'an, the capital of a mountainous coastal district in the remote northeast of Fukien Province. It was known throughout China for its tea production, the beautiful Baiyun Mountains, and its inviting nearby harbor nicknamed the "Golden Passage." It was a quite literary city, with proportionally more Government schools than other cities in Fukien. This meant much more competition for Mission schools, though the latter still had the edge in the education of girls.

More than four centuries earlier, Roman Catholic missionaries had begun work in Fu'an and continued to maintain a strong presence in the city. A Protestant presence that started ten years earlier had been overshadowed by the strong Catholic influence. As Sophie observed, they had "hundreds of adherents to our Anglican tens."[13] This situation was made worse by conflict between the city's three female Protestant missionaries. Although Bishop Hind had placed additional resources at their disposal, he needed an

13. S. S. Newton, Annual Letter, 24 August 1929, 2.

experienced missionary and deaconess to work alongside the new pastor to rebuild the fractured relationships among the female workers, and to make more headway in this highly Catholic and pagan environment.

From one point of view, Fu'an was a special place to work. As it was founded by the Dublin University Fukien Mission rather than CMS, she felt closer to the work of Robert and Louisa Stewart who had influenced so many of its missionaries to come. But, for several reasons, Sophie found Fu'an a difficult place to work.[14] This was partly due to the heavy brogue of its dialect making it difficult for her to be understood, but also due to the district's greater lawlessness and warlord intrusion. She had just settled in with a few basic possessions when bandit activity reached the city and martial law was declared. Several days later, eight brigands were shot on the bridge near the Western Gate where she loved to walk. Not long after, another four were executed as a deterrent to their comrades. In spite of these challenges, Sophie continued to lead services in the church, teach Scripture at the Girls School, and carry out evangelism in surrounding villages with a bible-woman. The Communist movement's influence in Fu'an was due to the proximity of Mao-Tse-tung's base in the neighboring province of Kwangsi. There was considerable sympathy for the new ideology among peasants, and the local warlord sometimes joined in Communist military sorties. Despite occasional attacks from Northern forces, Communist influence gradually expanded into northern Fukien, where a local warlord held considerable power.[15]

On one occasion while traveling in the countryside, Sophie found herself unexpectedly face-to-face with the young local warlord. In a confronting manner, he shouted "What are you doing here?"

Sophie replied, "I am here to tell the women in this village about the love of God."

He scoffed, "Why should anyone listen to you?"

"Because I have known this God all my life! I could tell you more about him if you are interested."

Looking at her disdainfully, he said, "Why should I listen to you when, unlike a good Chinese woman, you do not even wear trousers?"

She hoisted her skirt above her knees to show her pantaloons. "Oh yes I do!"

---

14. See further the *Church Missionary Gleaner* (Australia) 1 February, 1929.

15. On the background to this geographical shift in focus of the Communist Movement, see McDonald, *The Urban Origins*, 1978.

Taken back, he paused for several seconds, shrugged his shoulders and rode off.[16]

In July 1929, Sophie returned to Foochow and then took her annual summer break at Kuliang. It is interesting to speculate whether while she was in the capital and the mountain resort during the next few months, she might have heard or met the emerging local Christian Chinese church leader, Watchman Nee, who was beginning to set up his network of churches in Foochow and the surrounding region. Though he was more influenced by Methodism than Anglicanism, he embodied many of the strengths of Fukienese Christianity and gradually made Kuliang a key part of his expanding work.[17]

Towards the end of her time in Fu'an, she had a mishap that laid her up for several days. Tripping over a doorstep, she fell against a cupboard, and severely bruised her face and rib. This was countered by hearing that the CMS Conference had decided she could return to her old mission district. As she wrote home;

> I trust it may be the Master's will to let me stay a little time in the villages of Lieng Kong before I return to help at home. I want to see about finding some others to take up the work we must lay down.[18]

After settling back in her home in Lieng Kong compound, she began to carry out her plan to concentrate on strengthening believers; teaching the women together for short periods; and heightening Christian responsibility to neighbors.

---

16. This account is based on a story shared by one of Sophie's nieces who stayed with her from time to time in Woodford.

17. On Watchman Nee's connections with Foochow see further Roberts, *Understanding Watchman Nee*, 6–18, and Kinnear, *Against the Tide*, 1973.

18. *The Church Missionary Gleaner* (Australia), 1 October 1929, 10.

Sophie's mobile chair that she took on longer trips

As in earlier days, taking up her trusted stick and mobile chair, Sophie journeyed to surrounding villages. She received encouraging reports of some Christian women growing in their faith and the conversion of unbelieving husbands to whom they had been betrothed.

A special occasion was going to Daik-hok's home to give blessings to a second daughter. Maorong, who was six years old at the time, vividly remembered her visit.

> In the old days there were so few Westerners in China, so wherever those foreigners went, they always aroused much curiosity. On that day when my sister was born, Ngu Ma (Grandma Newton) came to our house, followed by a large crowd of Chinese men in the courtyard. Ngu Ma was old but looked so beautiful. She was dressed in elegant and graceful clothes, all in dark color. Seeing my father coming out of the room holding the baby, she smiled and teased him saying, 'Kö-sek se muoi.' (meaning 'Pity it's a girl', as in the old days people preferred boys to girls.) Now this surprised all

the guests even more! As they all murmured, 'Hey did you hear what she just said?' 'Why she speaks our language, just like us!'[19]

During her time in Lieng Kong, Sophie often thought back to her previous year in Fu'an. In the middle of March, she read the shocking news that a Communist force had crossed the border from an adjoining province into northern Fukien and had captured Fu'an. As a consequence, a majority of local officials and two thousand inhabitants lost their lives. After plundering parts of the town, the invading forces then retreated westwards across the border into the mountainous region of Kiangsi. Sophie might well have been one of the victims of this atrocity if CMS had asked her to stay in Fu'an for a second year.

By June 1930, armed unrest had increased so much in the more remote parts of Fukien that missionaries in these areas were ordered back to Foochow. In July, even as close to the capital as Kuliang, they heard rifle shots in the distance and the occasional pounding of heavier arms. As the situation grew more serious, they could "hear the machine guns, and supplies of food and wood are no longer able to come down the river."[20] Anxiety grew when news reached them of the abduction of two lady missionaries, Misses Nettleton and Harrison, by bandits not far from Fu'an. Their captors' demand for a ransom of US$100,000 came in the form of a note wrapped around one of the women's fingers, an incident that was widely reported, including the *New York Times* and *Time* magazine.[21] As soon as possible, Chinese troops were sent out to try and locate the women, and representatives of the British Consul and CMS collected the ransom money. Sadly, when they arrived at the meeting place they found that the bandits had already shot the women.

---

19. Maorong's account was relayed to us by our Chinese friend and local historian George Ngu.

20. S. S. Newton, *The Church Missionary Gleaner* (Australia), 1 October 1933, 11.

21. For the former see "Deaths of Missionaries," *New York Times*, 4 October 1930.

Letter from Sophie, reported in *The Church Missionary Gleaner*

In October 1930, the British Consul gave permission for missionaries to return to their districts. Sophie wrote:

> I return to Lieng Kong realising a sense of 'coming home'. I shall never cease to praise Him for giving happy times of fellowship with bible-women and other workers and Christians, many old pupils, children, and grandchildren to whom it has been a joy to minister, chiefly in the villages. In spite of limitations in strength and equipment, it has been fruitful and a comfort in my last year in China.[22]

During her final three months, as she made her farewells to many of her converts and co-workers, Sophie recalled the walk with Amy and Minna up to that ruined pagoda.

> In the beginning there were three of us, one Bible Woman, a few baptized women throughout the district, here and there one who had unbound her feet. There was no Hospital, no Women's or Girls' School. Our chief work was among a small number of Day Schools taught by many unsatisfactory Christians which owing to lack of proper supervision had to be closed . . . In spite of all mistakes, often through ignorance and trustfulness, God was with us, and the work grew by prayer, and the trials drove us more to Him. Now after 30 years we see all over the district little churches with small congregations, ministered to by a Catechist or Day School

22. S. S. Newton, Annual Letter, 12 September 1930, 3.

teacher, who conducts regular services on Sunday, and is often appealed to for advice and prayer in time of difficulty and sickness. We are always welcome and can stay as long as possible with them. Though Day Schools are less in number they are efficient and pleasant to visit. The staff of Bible Women is now nine, capable and earnestly doing faithful work all over the District, with whom we are in constant touch as real colleagues and can hold fellowship in work and prayer. And what shall I say about the Girls Boarding School. Words fail to express my thankfulness for all it has meant to Lieng Kong and elsewhere—good wives for Christians, and mothers to present pupils; a big band of teachers, including one girl studying in the Central Medical College; also of nurses, some in Hospitals and others marrying and opening up dispensaries in their own homes. Through this the status of women has been raised a hundredfold, while our Hospital continues to flourish and many grateful patients go home having heard the gospel.[23]

A Boys House had also been built in conjunction with the Girls' School, and there were now several branches of the Mothers' Union as well as the ongoing work of the Women's School.

In closing her last annual letter, Sophie indicated that she had decided to tender her resignation. While she would have liked to stay another year, the last two summers in Fukien had been more than she could bear. Her last few days are captured in a description from Miss Onyon.

After Miss Newton paid farewell visits to country centres, she came back to spend her last Christmas in this station. In consultation with my Chinese fellow-workers, I had decided to celebrate the 20th anniversary of the Girls School (which Miss Newton had started) by inviting as many of the old pupils as could come and spend Christmas and say farewell to Miss Newton, who had done so much for the School since its commencement. Almost 80 former pupils were present during part of the three days, which were given up to gatherings for pleasure and for devotional meetings.[24]

A final celebration took place at the city church in Lieng Kong. This took the form of a large and sumptuous banquet. As preparation for this, the following invitation was sent out.

Deaconess Ngu Huo-sek comes from the United Kingdom. So far she has worked in Lieng Kong as missionary for thirty-four years.

---

23. S. S. Newton, Annual Letter, 12 September 1930, 1–2.
24. Marion Onyan, Annual Letter, December, 1931.

This time, she will be returning to her country on retirement, and on the departing banquet there were endless tears of reluctance. On the second day of Christmas she will go to the Girls' School to bid goodbye. On January 2, a farewell meeting will be held at Lieng Kong Church. I, therefore, have composed a poem and a song, which are to be sung on that day with music and rhythm.

The poem expressed sadness at Sophie's leaving the city and district.

Sad rains falling, songs of farewell are breaking off the willow branches. The spring breeze is still blowing as ever, but who owns those apricot flowers? We remember there was a boat that came from the West, and how our teacher lived and toiled among us. Now all the sisters are at this party, with sorrow on our eyebrows.

The song expressed thankfulness for her work in Lieng Kong church and sadness at her leaving because she would be so misse.

Looking back to the establishment of Lieng Kong Church, we feel so blessed by the Lord, Who sent here Western missinaries to spread the Gospel and help save our heathen souls. From baby to toddler and to now, we thank the Lord for His many blessings, we thank the Lord for His many blessings.

We are fortunate to have Deaconess Ngu, who left her homeland for Lieng Kong, influencing and transforming all women in this region. Thirty-four years, and now she will be returning home on retirement. May our endless thoughts go with her.[25]

On the day she left, there was a sad farewell with her adoptive family. Having taught her "granddaughter" to knit during this last visit to Lieng Kong, Sophie promised that even though they would not be able to see each other, she would continue to send items she had knitted, such as warm woolen hats, as well as dresses that were hard to find in Fukien. That same day, there was also a heartfelt letter written in Chinese from the Church Committee that was given to deliver to her CMS Committee in Australia.

---

25. Introduction, Poem and Song from the Banks Family Collection.

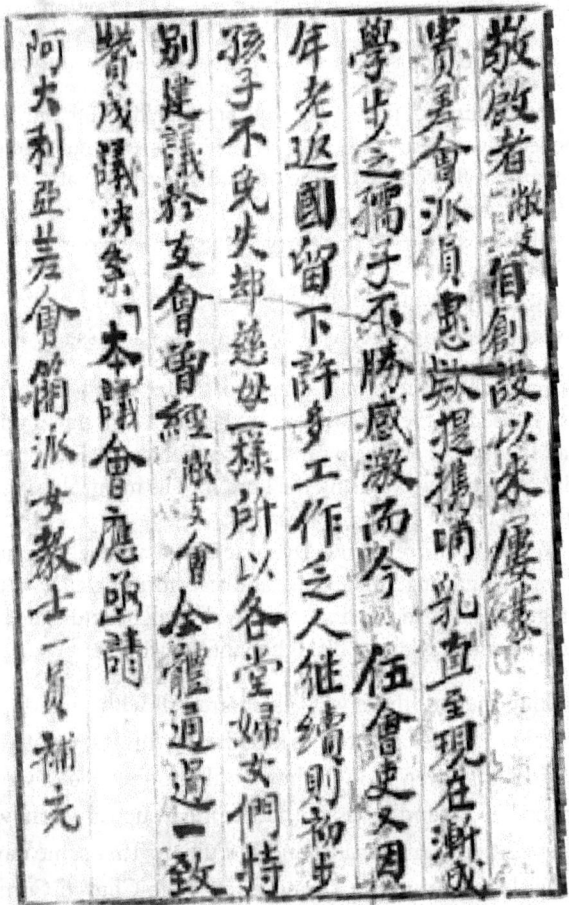

Original Chinese letter from Lieng Kong Church to CMS

January 7th 1931.

We reverently say that our Branch of the Church, from the beginning of its establishment has always received favours from you, the honourable Mother Church. You have always helped us in sending missionaries and giving money like a mother nourishing her child until now. We are growing up as a child learning to walk; so we all feel inexpressibly grateful.

But now, our dear Deaconess S.S. Newton returns to her country on account of her old age retirement. By this, her many kinds of work need somebody to continue them, or we, who are like a child learning the way, shall feel bereaved of a kind mother. Hence, we, all women, in every village church, suggested the following, specially before our Branch of the Church. And it has been agreed and passed by the whole Body of our Branch of the Church.

Our Council ought to earnestly ask our Mother Church in Australia to select and send one woman missionary to fill Deaconess S.S. Newton's vacancy, by coming to Lieng Kong to continue a woman's missionary work and to care for the women believers and unbelievers. And also we entrust Deaconess S.S. Newton to state and narrate for us before the important men of the Mother Church about the need of our Branch Church and our real earnest request for a worker.

Will your honourable Society look through this statement?

And we wish you peace in the Lord's doctrine,

Chung Hwa Sheng Kung Hwei
Council of the Branch Church
of Lieng Kong Fukien, South China
Chairman, Wang Zee Chwan, Secretary, Wou Moul Joon.[26]

---

26. Lieng Kong Church Council, "Letter to the Mother Church in Australia," 7 January 1931, in the Banks Family Collection.

8

Missing Her Adopted Land and Longing for a Heavenly Home

Having packed up all her possessions, Sophie left Lieng Kong for the very last time on 6 January 1931, just one calendar day short of the date that she had first left for China. As she had done so many times before, going first to Foochow to say goodbye to her friends and the bishop, and then going on to Hong Kong on 20 January she boarded the SS *Taiping* for home. So ended what Australian missionary historian Keith Cole describes as "thirty-four years of outstanding service in the cause of Christ in China."[1]

Sophie's first point of contact with Australia was a short stopover on Thursday Island, where she was able to attend the Memorial Church. While there, she broke a small bone in her foot, and her arrival in Sydney on 8 February was somewhat dramatic, hobbling down the gangplank with the aid of crutches to greet confused family and friends. After disembarking, she was interviewed by a Sydney journalist.

> Deaconess S.S. Newton, who for many years has been a missionary of the Church Missionary Society returned to Sydney by the Taiping yesterday. Miss Newton said that 34 years ago yesterday she landed in Foochow to take up the work of the Society, and the progress made in the Province of Fukien had been just like a dream . . . she carried with her a letter from the Chinese Church Council to the Church Missionary Society in Sydney requesting

---

1. Cole, *Church Missionary Society in Australia*, 144.

that someone should be sent out to fill the vacancy caused by her retirement.²

This article, accompanied by a photograph, gave Sophie top billing over one on a "young English aviatrix" planning a solo flight from England to Australia in an aeroplane presented to her by her wealthy father!

Much of 1931 was spent settling back into Australia, attending and speaking at CMS gatherings and Days of Prayer, visiting link churches, and enjoying time with friends and family. The Rt Rev John Wright, Archbishop of Sydney, renewed her deaconess license so she could take part in services where she could assist a clergyman or officiate when none was available.³

For Sophie, settling back in Woodford in her little "Isleham" cottage after four and a half years was both a delight and a challenge. Initially there was just so much to do. She had brought some cane furniture back with her and soon began to decorate the cottage with Chinese artifacts—scrolls in Chinese letters, her portable chair, and a long walking stick presented to her in Lieng Kong City as a respected elder. Over the years, these objects inevitably led to conversations about China and about the gospel with many who came into the house. Keen to live as simply as she had in China during these Depression-affected years, Sophie soon had a vegetable garden growing on her large block of land.

Life in Woodford in the early 1930s would probably be described today as "rustic," but to Sophie, having lived with deprivation and hard work for most of her life, it was modern and well equipped. Typically, homes in Woodford at the time had a fuel stove in the kitchen for cooking and boiling water for bathing, an open fire in the lounge room to help cope with cold winters, and a pan toilet down the backyard. Unlike most homes in that area, "Isleham" also had a small storage room and a back verandah. Sophie would have purchased most of her grocery needs at the local general store. There was a butcher and baker in the adjoining suburb of Hazelbrook, and for any additional shopping, it was only a fifteen minute train ride to the larger town of Katoomba. With a population of fewer than three hundred, all letters and parcels had to be collected from the Woodford Post Office, which became something of a meeting place for locals.⁴ A repairman from the area, who charged her very modest rates, helped Sophie with the maintenance of the house.

2. *The Sydney Morning Herald*, 9 February 1931, 4.
3. J. Wright, Letter to S. S. Newton, 13 February 1931.
4. See generally, Goodlet, *Hazelbrook and Woodford*, which was written by a later

St Paul's Anglican Church, Woodford, in the 1930s

梁劉柔芬

Towards the end of a very busy 1931, as she was settling into her new life and work in Woodford, Sophie wondered how she could continue to serve her beloved China now that she had left it behind. An important way of doing this was regularly praying over, writing letters to, and making presents, for her growing adopted family there. She also knitted small caps for her "grandchildren," that were lovingly received and worn by them.

Another way of serving China resulted in a visit to Sydney in August by Howard Mowll, the Anglican Bishop of West China, and his wife Dorothy. She was the daughter of Rev John Martin, with whom Sophie had stayed on first arriving in Foochow. Since he was a widower, she had often helped look after Dorothy and his two other children. After Dorothy returned to China as a CMS missionary in 1915, serving in Szechwan, the two of them had met up at an educational conference, as well as Howard at a China-wide Christian conference in Shanghai in 1923 after he and Dorothy had married. Meeting up with the Mowlls during their visit to Sydney was propitious, as a year later he was invited to become the next Archbishop of Sydney, a position he held till 1956.[5] Dorothy found Sophie one of the few people in Sydney who understood her love of China.

CMS missionary. Also relevant is "St Paul's Church Woodford," 60–63.

5. After the Boxer Rebellion, CMS and CIM missionaries in the more remote western

The day after Howard Mowll's enthronement at St Andrew's Cathedral on 13 March 1934 and the civic reception in the Town Hall, Sophie attended a garden party in the grounds of Bishopscourt hosted by Dorothy. A few weeks later, the Mowlls came up to Woodford to spend the day with her, and a few months later, they came to stay for a week. Over the next 20 years, right up to their deaths within a year of each other, the Mowlls visited Sophie regularly, sometimes combining these visits with official church business, sometimes when speaking at a conference in the area, and sometimes when on vacation. Often they stayed nearby for their annual holiday. For Sophie, these visits were like "going home" and were greatly cherished.

Five years after her return, as she was nearing seventy, Sophie retired from her formal role as a deaconess in the parish. While this relieved her of the responsibility of leading services and preaching, she continued to serve the church in Woodford for the next 15 years. She also kept up her monthly CMS Prayer Meetings in the city, traveling on one of the two steam trains that served the mountains.

In the latter half of 1936, some unexpected and wonderful news came her way. Her cousin Joan and husband George Hall (a member of the philanthropic family behind the Walter and Eliza Hall Trust) had made bookings to travel by ship to England for the coronation of King George VI and Queen Elizabeth, following the abdication of Edward VIII. Finding themselves unable to go, Joan offered Sophie one of their tickets. She jumped at the chance to see her birthplace, visit relatives and friends from China, and tour some of the countryside. Since only her fares to and from England were covered, she wrote to relatives and missionaries, who immediately offered her places to stay in Kent and Buckinghamshire.

In the New Year, shortly before her trip began, Sophie attended the annual CMS Summer School in the adjoining township of Lawson.[6] She then boarded the *SS Oronsay* on 13 February to begin her year-long overseas trip. On the way, the boat called in at Colombo, Port Said, and Gibraltar, before docking in Southampton on 24 March. Although it was cold, she was thrilled to be back in the land of her birth and there were friends from China to meet her. "How my heart bounds with deep gratitude," she

---

provinces became the subjects of attack by lawless groups and hostile crowds with increasing frequency. The Mowlls were no exception to this, and several times they found themselves in dangerous situations. See further Loane, *Archbishop Mowll*, and "Dorothy Ann Mowll," 271–72.

6. Recorded in Lambert, *Parish of Lawson*, 61.

said, "for all the [ways] He has so graciously led me."⁷ The day after her arrival, Sophie went up to London and spent a few days visiting the main sites—London Bridge, Trafalgar Square, Buckingham Palace, Westminster Abbey, and Greenwich Observatory. She also went to CMS House and met up with some of the people there.

A copy of the Coronation program

The first significant event Sophie attended, on 12 May, was the coronation itself. Before it was light, she went with her relatives by car into London. They then walked to their seats in the viewing stands at Hyde Park, just ten rows from the front. Thousands of people had turned up before midnight and slept on newspaper sheets until dawn. As an observer from the UK recorded:

7. This, and following quotations, come from Circular Letters written during this trip.

> From a building on the other side of the road, a loud speaker tells us that the King and Queen are leaving Buckingham Palace to go to Westminster Abbey. Cheers can be heard, the day has begun. As each important thing takes place we are told about it from this loud speaker. The procession, the Abbey ceremony, the oath and finally 'He is crowned,' 'Long live the King' . . .
>
> Then we were informed that they were leaving the Abbey and would soon be in Hyde Park. Long hours of waiting and then the first troops appeared. Mounted bands, beautiful horses, colorful uniforms, and well-rifled troops. Men in red coats, gold braid, black trousers, in the blue, the gray. Men from as far away as the British Empire reaches . . . The Royal troops from India, South Africa, New Zealand, Australia, Canada, Egypt. The Turks, Arabians and all the Scottish, Welsh and native land, sea, and air forces.
>
> And finally came the Royal coaches with Queen Mary, the Princesses, Dukes, Duchesses, Lords and Ladies, the Prime Minister, the King's Guards, and the King and Queen. There in his royal coach, dressed in his royal robes, scepter in his hand, his queen by his side, was King George VI and Queen Elizabeth. A great cheer went up.[8]

Towards the end of June, Sophie also attended a Garden Party at Lambeth Palace. Near the end of July, she set off for Keswick in the glorious Lake District in the north of England. She had first heard about the annual convention that took place there during George Grubb's mission in 1891, and many of her CMS co-workers, along with Howard and Dorothy Mowll, had been deeply influenced by the Keswick Movement. Her letters home provided a full account of this once-in-a-lifetime opportunity—the 3000-strong meetings, various trips into the countryside when there was free time, and a mass celebration of the Lord's Supper that concluded the convention.

In September Sophie managed to visit her birthplace, Isleham, not far from Cambridge, of which she had only dim childhood memories. It was also the burial place of her older brother George, who died when she was three. As there were several cemeteries in the now sprawling village, it took her two days to find his grave. She arrived during the celebration of the annual Harvest Festival, and in the afternoon of the festival she addressed and assisted with a special service for women and girls. During the evening service, in which she assisted, she donated a new cover for the font that she had made during her time in England. Sophie then visited the three places

8. "The Coronation of King George VI," 21 May 2010.

in Cambridge where she had stayed as a child, as well as King's College where Howard Mowll had studied.

Next came one of the highlights of her trip, reconnecting with Amy Wilkinson, one of her first two co-workers in Lieng Kong District. "O how we talked of the past! the present! and the future. We seemed to live in China . . ." Together they told and retold stories of the adventures they had shared—living in their small house, working in the dispensary, visiting the far-flung villages, building the Girls School and the church, as well as coping with the challenges of typhoons, floods, cholera, and evacuations. They dwelt particularly on the day they climbed the hill to the ruined pagoda where the three of them surveyed the district and divided up the work. Later that week she accompanied Amy to the docks in London where she worked among sailors from Fukien who loved to hear someone so far from home speaking their dialect. "I have had a most delightful week with my dear old colleague of Lieng Kong days", she wrote home. Next she visited the China Institute and met with more than twenty of China's hand-picked young men doing advanced study in universities and colleges in England. She found them "so keen, so clever and, thank God, quite a number are earnest Christians." Later she visited and stayed with Marion Onyon, on furlough from Lieng Kong, and from their time together she concluded that "At present, there is a wide-open opportunity. Labourers are few—especially men!"

In early October 1937, Sophie prepared to leave for Palestine. She had already contacted the headquarters of the Mission to the Jews in London, with which she had been involved since 1900. When she arrived in Haifa she was met by a member of the Mission who arranged visits to many of the sacred sites in Jerusalem. Sophie sometimes found it hard to believe she was walking in the very places Jesus himself had walked. She also saw places linked to Mission to the Jews projects for which she had coordinated funds, such as a Christian hospital for Jews, Jewish translation of the New Testament, and a school in which a student had been supported.

On 13 December, she boarded a ship for Australia. Serendipitously, a shipboard companion turned out to be Miss Hassall, a member of the wider family of Eliza Hassall, with whom she had studied at Marsden Training Home before first leaving for China. On 15 December they crossed the Equator, called in at Fremantle just after New Year, and arrived in Sydney on 13 January 1938. In many respects this overseas trip brought Sophie's life full circle, enabling her to reconnect with the land of her birth, renew links with some of her co-workers from China, and fulfil a long-time dream to visit Palestine.

梁劉柔芬

Archbishop Howard and Dorothy Mowll on overseas trip

Upon her return, Sophie was invited by the Mowlls to join a "Pray for China" group that met monthly in the city. The major impetus for the group's formation was the worsening situation in China, which was facing significant internal and external threats. In some places, Communist sympathizers were actively targeting Christians, subjecting them to public insult, beatings and destruction of their homes. Meanwhile, Japan had begun to invade China from both the north and the east. Not long after Sophie's return to Australia, the Mowlls received a telegram for this prayer group from none other than General Chiang Kai-Shek.

> Our nation is fighting not only to protect our national independence, but also to preserve world peace and justice. This is recognized by the people of the world who believe in righteousness. As you meet for prayer think of the suffering of your countrymen, the safety of the nation, the spirit of peace and love of Jesus Christ. Your faith will surely be accepted by God because righteousness cannot forever be destroyed or the light of peace extinguished in the world. This is my firm belief. I appreciate very much your patriotic spirit and the deep sympathy of our foreign friends. As I send these greetings to you, my hope is that you are one with

me in the determination to continue to the end in the struggle for truth and righteousness.⁹

Early one morning in January 1939, Sophie's brother-in-law, Henry Glanville, rang to tell her that "dear Grace" had died suddenly. As Sophie put down the phone, an image of Grace looking a picture of health at the recent family Christmas get-together came to mind. Her funeral was a marvelous testimony to her loving and sacrificial ministry to a wide range of people, not only in the church but in the wider community, especially the poor and needy. For Sophie, her death was a huge blow, only softened by her knowledge that Grace was now in the most loving hands. Towards the end of the year, she received a postcard from a cousin in England, Squadron Leader Edward Newton, written just before heading off to war, with the news that the aunt she had stayed with on her recent trip to England had passed away peacefully.

It was not long before towns in the Blue Mountains began to feel the practical impact of the Second World War. Food rationing was introduced for tea, sugar, meat, and butter, although locals were able to provide some of their own butter and meat and so were less affected than those in the city. As was her practice during the Great War, Sophie prayed regularly for members of her extended family in military service in various parts of the world. In early June 1941, Sophie lost another close family member. Her sister Amy's health had been slowly deteriorating to the point where, despite her not being allowed into the house for years, Sophie was unexpectedly asked back to "Ormskirk" in Burwood to nurse her. After a month, Amy passed away.

In September, Sophie had a further opportunity to connect with people serving in China. At the request of Howard Mowll, Bishop C.T. Song, his indigenous successor in Western Szechwan, was invited to give three public addresses on "Church History and Philosophy" in Sydney at St Andrew's Cathedral. Bishop Song was a scholarly man who had studied in Cambridge, and his wife was the daughter of Bishop Ding in Fukien.¹⁰ His stay at Bishopscourt for several weeks enabled Sophie opportunity to catch up on news about his family and China more generally. She was encouraged to hear that the Nationalist Government had regained some control

---

9. This was recorded in *The Unfinished Task of China*.

10. We have recounted parts of Bishop Song's story, together with a brief biography, in our book *Children of the Massacre*, especially 168–70.

over previously Japanese-occupied areas in the south-eastern part of the country, including Foochow and its surrounding districts.

October 1942 was a special month, marking 50 years since God had first challenged Sophie to go to China through the visit of Robert Stewart and Eugene Stock. The event was marked by the opening of its new headquarters of the NSW CMS next door to the Anglican Cathedral in Sydney. A year later, an expansion of the talk given at this event in the first history of the Society's work featured a frontispiece photo of Sophie playing the harmonium with the school girls' choir in Deng-doi![11]

During the War, Sophie often extended hospitality to people coming up from the city.

> My house has been honored all through the years by visits from Archbishops, Bishops, Archdeacons, Canons, and many clergy, as well as missionaries from China, India, Africa, Egypt, Japan, Palestine and Hebrew Christians, and of course many from our own beloved homeland.[12]

In November 1944, Woodford was the epicenter of one of the destructive bushfires that occasionally swept through parts of the Blue Mountains. With flames enveloping the town, sixteen homes in Woodford were destroyed in just over an hour, their occupants escaping with only the clothes they were wearing. Although the fire came up the valley below the ridge on which her house was built, seventy-seven year old Sophie and her home were mercifully spared from this disaster. After the fire had died down, Sophie helped in the distribution of relief through St Paul's Church and of funds made available by Archbishop Mowll.

During the latter years of the war, one of Amy's grandchildren, Audrey, often spent the weekend, and sometimes longer, at "Isleham."

> I vividly remember the house and the 'trading table' in the living room on which visitors and guests placed odds and ends, jams, plants, books etc. These items were then either purchased by such people or sold elsewhere so that the money could be sent to support mission work in China . . . I will never forget the little garments Auntie was continually crocheting for babies in Chinese villages. They were very shapeless and one wondered how they were received . . .

---

11. Johnstone, *Australian Church Missionary Society,* Frontispiece.

12. S. S. Newton, "Dedication of Newton Cottage." This, and other unascribed documents in this chapter come from the Banks Family Collection.

I also remember a woman at the Woodford Academy next door who had a dairy from whom Auntie used to buy milk in a little aluminium can to make her own butter. The frugal habits established by her years in China remained with her all her life and the biscuits she made from rancid butter were not palatable even to us hungry young people.

She also had a very direct, humorous side. After a service in the local church she commented "how hysterically bad the preaching of some men is!" I most of all remember how much she lived and breathed Christianity, which was the centre of her life. When Auntie was talking about such things, it was as if Jesus was sitting right beside her. She just glowed. She has been a very big influence on my life.[13]

At this time, Sophie deepened her friendship with Reverend F. B. Dillon and his family. She had first met Reverend Dillon when he was at Lawson a decade earlier, and now he was a rector at St Hilda's Church of England at Katoomba. When there was no service at Woodford, Sophie would often attend St Hilda's, where she also got to know Reverend Dillon's young son, Howard, who went on to become a leading clergyman in the diocese. Howard sometimes visited Sophie with his father and remembered her "as an unassuming, lively, older lady with wispy hair. I admired her for her missionary service and her commitment to prayer—always kneeling when engaged in it. I also well remember a box in which people put requests for prayer."[14]

Another young person, David Claydon, who later became Federal Secretary of CMS in Australia, also remembered visiting her with his aunt Lora. "Sophie offered us a cup of tea and I watched her as she poured the 'hot' water out of a hot water bottle she took out of her bed into the cups—I have never forgotten that incident."[15]

梁劉柔芬

With the formal surrender by Japan on 2 September 1945, Australia and the rest of the world, including China, were finally able to return to "normal." The following year Sophie attended the Deaconess Institute's

13. Audrey Ridley, recorded interview, 17 January 2011.
14. Canon Howard Dillon, in conversation with Robert Banks, February 2002.
15. David Claydon, personal correspondence with Robert and Linda Banks, January 2012.

50th-anniversary celebration of recognized training in the Sydney Diocese at a Deaconess House reunion in Newtown. It was a wonderful day of catching up with old co-workers and friends, having a photographic record taken of the occasion, and hearing the most recent news about China from the lips of Mary Andrews who, having endured the hardships of the Japanese occupation, had recently returned. Sophie was pleased that "peace in our time" also meant more time with the Mowlls, who throughout the war had been busily engaged with various projects to help the people of Sydney. She liked to keep in touch with what was happening in China, and a visit from Mrs Mowll bringing Bishop Song and his son, who was studying at the University of Sydney, in 1947 was a special treat.

Deaconess Reunion—Sophie Newton, front row, 3rd from left

On 11 September 1947, Sophie celebrated her 80th birthday. Until now she had been able to manage the upkeep of "Isleham," but now she could no longer keep up her garden and it was no longer possible to find people to do occasional work for a reasonable sum. Over the next two years, news of the growing number of Communist successes in the civil war raging in China concerned her, and she was deeply disappointed when after their victory all missionaries were expelled from the country.

Towards the end of 1951, she decided to gift "Isleham" to CMS. Arrangements were made for the dedication of Newton Cottage, as it was to be called, to take place on 28 June 1952.

At 11.30am on a beautiful sunny day about 50 people met to dedicate this 26 year old cottage to the glory of God, and for the use of others instead of its present owner ... the little service was opened by the Hon. Treasurer of CMS, Mr Dakin, who gave the reason for our gathering. I then spoke and told them that this was a very glad day for me and that I rejoice and praise God for all it means as we dedicate this God-given house for the use of missionaries on furlough, the CMS family and those interested in overseas mission fields ... I leave it now deeply thankful to God for all the joy and pleasure, rest and relaxation it has given to me, the privilege of taking services in the dear little church and sharing in the work of the parish with those who have been good friends to me since I came among them. And now I wait 'till He calls' or 'till He comes.'[16]

A photo of Sophie taken in 1930 just as she left China, was hung over the fireplace in the cottage, accompanied by a few words about her entrusting it to CMS.

She then moved into "Kendall House," a CMS home for missionaries in Strathfield, only a short 15-minute ride by train into the city. One advantage of the move was being able to attend meetings of the Pray for China group more regularly, especially when it was grappling with the fallout of the ultimate Communist expulsion of all missionaries from China. Since her 60th anniversary of becoming a deaconess in the Sydney Diocese was approaching, in November Archbishop Mowll organized a Service of Celebration in her honor at St Andrew's Cathedral. The event was well attended by friends, supporters, fellow deaconesses, ex-parishioners, and others who had benefited from her ministry over the years. The Archbishop spoke about Sophie's life and work, highlighting from personal experience her contribution as a woman of prayer. This was followed by a luncheon where she spoke to her fellow deaconesses.

Sophie began her speech by saying "how very humble and greatly honoured" she felt. What most stood out in her years of service was "God's loving patience, forbearance, protection and provision."[17] Her address dwelt first on the key words the apostle Paul uses to describe Phoebe—"sister", "servant" and "helper" (Romans 16:1-2), adding compelling examples of ways these qualities were exemplified in people she had known.

---

16. S.S. Newton, "Dedication of Newton Cottage," The General Secretary of CMS, Rev (later Bishop) Clive Kerle, formally thanked her in writing for "the great value" of the cottage to the Society.

17. S. S. Newton, "Phoebe—The Model Deaconess."

One example was a nurse who got up several hours before her shift to bathe Sophie when she was ill in hospital. She went on to explain that following in Phoebe's footsteps involved lifelong devotion to the Lord Jesus and determination to encourage all professing Christians to witness for Christ. Towards the end of the talk, she told a typically self-deprecating, humorous story about a woman who had never prayed before in public doing so for the first time. When asked about how she had gathered the courage to do this, the woman replied: "When I heard Miss Sophie pray I thought I could do as well as that and tried!"

Sophie found her life at Kendall House a challenge. Most difficult was having so little freedom and room in an institution run by others. One day when Archbishop Mowll was visiting, in her usual direct way she said that she was not enjoying the place and would prefer to be with the Lord. Fixing his eyes on her, he replied firmly, "Sophie, that one thing is out of your control. You will die when God wants you to and not before."[18] She accepted the reproof and did not talk this way again. But his remarks helped her to realize that God still had a purpose for her.

> Now my work is Prayer and Intercession, and I am learning about it more especially as it is a lonely piece of work. So far I have not found a kindred spirit to bear the burden with me.

梁劉柔芬

In the middle of June 1954, Sophie transferred from "Kendall House" to "Arrawatta," another CMS home in nearby Chatswood. There she continued to entertain occasional guests, some of them high-ranking—such as the Consul General for Korea, as well as her usual visits from friends like the Mowlls and others. From this point on she kept a notebook in which she recorded, on one side of the page, who and what she prayed for, and on the other, answers to prayer. Its pages contained references to numerous people, organizations, and circumstances in Australia and overseas.

The following year, 1956, her remaining three siblings—John, Herbert, and Florence—all died. With the passing of this older generation, she decided to focus more on the younger one.

One of these, Lawrence Banks, wrote:

> I found her kindly and gracious, clear in mind and crisp in speech. She offered me tea and biscuits and asked me if I had been

18. This was noted in her Prayer Diary for 1954–58.

confirmed. I said 'not yet'. Looking back, the strongest thing I recall was the way she talked about her faith. She told me that she was looking forward to 'going home' to be with God. The way she said this sounded like she knew what she was talking about.[19]

(It was interesting to discover after her death 18 months later, that among the papers both Lawrence's and Robert's names were found in her Prayer Diary).

In September 1956, Sophie heard to her delight that the Mowlls were able to visit China as part of a church delegation, even though Dorothy was suffering from advanced Hodgkin's Disease. After their return, Sophie was able to catch up on how the church in China, now firmly under Communist rule, was faring. The following year, Mary Andrews, now principal of Deaconess House, encouraged a young student deaconess to spend time with Sophie before she left for the mission field. Olive (who with her husband Harry Cotter had a long and distinguished ministry with CMS in Africa and Australia) visited her in her bedsitter several times that year. She recalled Sophie's response to strangers, interest in Olive's life and activities, and indicators of her relationship with God.

> On her train trips to and from CMS meetings in the City, even though they were no more than 15 minutes long, she would always try and start a conversation about Jesus with people next to her . . .
>
> From the outset she showed a great interest in what was happening to me, and my work. I learned a great deal from her about 'how you could keep serving God right up into your grey hairs' . . .
>
> In between our get-togethers Sophie would write and ask whether her prayers for me had been answered . . . and saying (in one of their last meetings) though my eyes are going, I see Him more clearly every day.[20]

---

19. Lawrence Banks, in a recorded interview, 8 March 2012.
20. Olive Cotter, recorded interview. 12 February 2011.

The last photograph of Sophie, aged 90

On 23 December, Dorothy Mowll finally went "safely home." The following year, Sophie's own health began to decline, and she was finally moved to the "Home of Peace," another deaconess institution a couple of suburbs away, where one of the Claydon girls, Frieda, was matron. There, on 24 July 1957, aged ninety, she died of a stroke. The next day, *The Sydney Morning Herald* reported her death under the headline "Oldest Woman Missionary Dies." It described her as the seventh person to go as a CMS missionary overseas, her being stationed in Foochow, her survival of the Boxer Rebellion, and her more than thirty-year service there. Reverend Geoff Fletcher, General Secretary of CMS, led the service and Archbishop Mowll gave the eulogy. About two hundred people, many of them committed CMS supporters, attended the service. It was, said Olive Cotter, "a wonderful occasion, with a strong sense of 'Hallelujah' about it."[21] Sophie was buried, with no headstone, alongside the grave of her beloved mother Emma at St Thomas' Enfield.

Throughout her life, Sophie always had difficulty knowing exactly where her home was. For a short time it was England; from infancy to early adulthood, Australia; then China, until she retired. Finally, apart

21. In the recorded interview with her mentioned above.

from a brief visit to England, again Australia. Emotionally, however, it was with China that she felt the closest connection. The uncertainty and the sense that she had no firm roots in any one place is typical of what missiologists describe as "international Christians." Sophie had lived in three continents, each of which was in some sense "home." At a deeper level, however, she lived, moved and had her being on a Fourth Continent made up of believers from many people groups, languages, and nations (Revelation 5:9). She was one of those "who were still living by faith when they died . . . aliens and strangers on earth. People who say such things show that they are looking for . . . a better country—a heavenly one. Therefore, God is not ashamed to be called their God, for he has prepared a city for them" (Hebrews 11:13–16).

In her last few years, Sophie increasingly looked forward to that city which would exceed her cherished memories of the village of Isleham, mission complex in Lieng Kong, and her peaceful cottage in Woodford. She longed to be reunited with her family and friends, colleagues and converts, in God's new world. Above all, she yearned to be with Jesus her Lord and see Him face-to-face.

Postlude

Becoming Part of the Ongoing Story

Our first trip to mainland China had been a mixture of curiosity and uncertainty as to what we would find in churches and Christian organizations. Having followed our grandaunt's story through written records, we were now able to retrace her actual footsteps. How many traces of her presence would survive from over a century earlier? Would we be able to find anyone who had a direct link with her? What would be the attitude of the people we met who, until relatively recently, had been largely separated from the rest of the world? All we knew at this stage was that God had set things up for us to visit the main places associated with Sophie's time in China.

Everyone we had met local pastors, historians, municipal officials, translators and guides, and church members—welcomed us, went out of their way to help, and made us feel at home. All showed interest in her story, seeing it as part of their own history as well. During later visits, we had some surprising experiences. In Fuzhou, we visited the campus of the City's school that Sophie helped relocate to the site that now houses the province's most important educational institution, Fuzhou Normal University. The school itself has since become the University's co-educational high school and therefore its chief entry point Our chief guide, a retired professor, turned out to be the son of the leading doctor at Tak-Ding Hospital, who had treated Sophie for severe bouts of migraine.

We also travelled to Liangjang district to visit the village where Sophie first served. A large TSPM church now stands on the site of the original building she and her co-workers had helped construct. In the district capital, the City Council plans to turn the dilapidated two-storey wooden Ladies' House where Sophie and her co-workers lived into the a historical museum. We were asked if we could provide some material for inclusion in a section on early missionaries. Next to the old house, a modern multi-storey building now serves as the headquarters of the officially-recognized TSPM churches in the district. This contains both a chapel and conference centre.

At Guliang, in the mountains above Fuzhou, we were invited to be present in a so-called Restoration Celebration. This marked the first stage of its development by the capital's Municipal Council into a major tourist attraction. The town remains a strong Christian center in the province with an unexpectedly large church building.

During our visits to Fujian, we learned something about the pervasive influence of bible-women on the church in the province, indeed in China more generally, over the preceding century. Since Sophie was involved first-hand in the training of several hundred such women, this deepened the extent of her legacy. These women were the main agents of conversion, and at times revival, among the people. After she left China, they continued to influence the next generation of male Christian leaders, which resulted in the church becoming more self-governed. During the first decades of Communist rule, they helped sustain the survival of Christianity and, when many male pastors were imprisoned, took up leadership roles in the church. This explains why there are so many female pastors not only in the province but in congregations throughout China today.

It was encouraging to hear the most recent official information on church growth in the areas where Sophie worked. In and around Dongdoichen, the tiny congregation she helped start has grown into five Government-registered churches with many thousands of members, as well as a large network of unregistered churches. In Liangjang district, the several small congregations of Sophie's day have expanded into fifty-five recognized congregations with around sixty thousand attenders, as well as around two hundred and fifty independent churches. In Guliang, a large percentage of the local population is Christian, many influenced by Watchman Nee's time there. In the capital, Fuzhou, and its surrounding region, the handful of churches from Sophie's early days has grown to around three hundred recognized churches and two thousand recognized meeting points, servicing a third of a million members. The area is also home to a range of unregistered grassroots churches.

POSTLUDE: BECOMING PART OF THE ONGOING STORY

In Fujian Province overall, unofficial estimates suggest that around fifteen percent of the population is Christian, one of the highest concentrations in China. The main training institution is Fuzhou Theological Seminary, whose expansive new premises on Nantai Island we were able to visit. On property provided by the provincial Government, this has the capacity to train three hundred male and female students, a large chapel, and a substantial library. The latter includes a room containing books in English donated by the United Bible Society, and a bay of books given in Sophie's memory from our personal theological collection. When we were shown this, the Vice-President of the seminary said: "We want you to know that this means part of you is always here with us."

One of the facilitators of this visit was a young woman we first met while speaking to students in the Chinese Department at Trinity Theological College in Singapore. As we were winding up our talk on early missionaries in Fujian, one student began to weep. On asking her afterwards whether we had said something distressing, she said "it was because you were telling part of the story of my own home church in Liangjang which I knew nothing about." After her return to China, she gained a position at Fuzhou Theological Seminary.

It was also fascinating to learn that Christians who migrated overseas from Fujian province have started Chinese churches throughout Southeast Asia, in places as distant as Singapore and Sydney. In other words, they have moved from being recipients to instruments of mission.

Over the last few years, we were able to make two further trips to Fujian and were only prevented from making more by the onset of the pandemic. Both visits provided opportunities to discover other aspects of Sophie's work and deepen our understanding of her contribution. We were finally able to locate the ancient pagoda which played such a key part in her story, and able to stand where she and her colleagues surveyed their district. We were also taken to the site of the church in Fuzhou that she occasionally attended, as well as the historic Three Lanes and Seven Alleys area surrounding it. During this trip, we were invited to meet staff and postgraduate students of a small Centre for Christian Studies in the Sociology Department of Fuzhou Normal University, the main tertiary institution in the province. This led to Rob being invited to give a seminar to a round forty postgraduate students on Sophie's life and work.

The highlight of this visit was the opportunity to meet with the first daughter of Sophie's adoptive family. In her early nineties, Mrs Chen

Maoring invited us to her home where, with a few family members, she shared personal stories about her "grandma." She talked about her father's persecution for his link with British missionaries, banishment to a labor camp during the Cultural Revolution, and death in 1972. However, "all through the hard times," she declared, "I kept the faith in my heart." On our last trip to Fuzhou, Maoring brought her entire extended family—around two-dozen people, most of them Christians—to meet us. In the reception area of the hotel where we were staying, we shared refreshments they had brought, exchanged gifts and, through translation, heard many more stories. At the conclusion of the meeting she said, in words that still ring in our ears, "if grandma had not adopted my father and aunt, none of these people here would have existed!" It was with much sadness that during the final preparation of this book we heard of Maorong's death shortly after her 100th birthday.

Sophie's legacy, then, is not just in surviving physical structures, or in the flourishing of Christianity in Fuzhou and Liangjang, but in a group of people to whom we are in some sense related, indeed part of our own wider family. And the more we have visited China, the more we have had the sense that rather than us helping to keep her story alive, we have been drawn into her ongoing work in the country she loved.

Bibliography

Primary Documents

Banks Family Collection: S. S. Newton's Autobiographical Fragments, Letters, Journals, Papers, Records, Photos, Prayer Book, and Prayer Diary.

Berry, D. M. *The Sister Martyrs of Kucheng: Memoirs and Letters of Eleanor and Elizabeth Saunders*. Melbourne: Melvin, Cullen & Slade, 1895. Reprinted in London by James A. Nisbet, 1895.

Church Missionary Society Archives, Central Records, East Asia General Japan and China. https://www.amdigital.co.uk/primary-sources/church-missionary-society-archive/.31.

Cole, E. Keith. *Letters from China 1893–1895: The Story of the Sister Martyrs of Kucheng*, St Hilary's, Kew, Melbourne, 1988.

Church Missionary Auxiliary (later Society) Australia: Annual Reports, Instructions to Missionaries, CMS Gleaner (Australia).

"The Coronation of King George VI." 21 May 2010. Viewed 24 March 2012, http://atruelifelovestory.blogspot.com.au/2010/05/coronation-of-king-george-vi/html

Welch, Ian, ed. "Amy Oxley: Letters from China—An Australian Missionary Nurse of the Church Missionary Association of New South Wales, Fujian Province, China, 1895–c1920." 2006. Viewed 20 March 2012, www.anglicanhistory.org/asia/china/welch_oxley.

Secondary Sources

"A Solitary Way." Melbourne: Valley Brothers, n.d.

Arndell, R. M. *Pioneers of Portland Head: Early Settlers of the Hawkesbury and Hunter Rivers and Squatters of North-Western New South Wales and Southern Queensland*. Cattai: n. p., 1973.

Banks, Linda, and Robert Banks. *'They Shall See His Face': The Story of Amy Oxley Wilkinson and Her Visionary Blind School in China*. Melbourne: Acorn, 2016. Rev. ed., Eugene, OR: Pickwick Publications, 2021.

———. *Through the Valley of the Shadow: Australian Women in War-Torn China*. Studies in Chinese Christianity. Eugene, OR: Pickwick Publications, 2019.

BIBLIOGRAPHY

Banks, Robert. "Hume, Eliza More." In *Australian Dictionary of Evangelical Biography*, edited by Brian Dickey, 176–77. Sydney: Evangelical History Association, 1994. https://sites.google.com › view › australian-dictionary-of-evangelical-biography

———. *Paul's Idea of Community: Spirit and Culture in the Early House Churches*. Grand Rapids: Baker, 2020.

Banks, Robert, and Linda Banks. *Children of the Massacre: The Extraordinary Story of the Stewart Family in Hong Kong and West China*. Eugene OR: Pickwick Publications, 2021.

Barclay, G. R, et al. *The Way of Partnership: With the CMS in China*. London: CMS, 1937.

Barnes, I. H. *Behind the Great Wall: The Story of CEZMS Work and Workers in China*. London: Marshall, 1896.

Bard, E. *The Chinese at Home*. London: Newnes, 1906.

Bays, Daniel H. *A New History*. Oxford: Blackwell, 2012.

Blainey, Geoffrey. *Black Kettle and Full Moon: Daily Life in a Vanished Australia*. Melbourne: Viking, 2003.

Borthwick, Sally "Schooling and Society in the Late Qing China." PhD diss., Australian National University, 1978.

Bossen, Laurel, and Hill Gates. *Bound Feet, Young Hands: Tracking the Demise of Footbinding in Village China*. Stanford: Stanford University Press, 2017.

Broomhall, Marshall, ed. *The Chinese Empire: A General and Missionary Survey*. London: China Inland Mission, 1907.

———. *Martyred Missionaries of the China Inland Mission*. London: Morgan & Scott/ China Inland Mission, 1902.

Chang, Jung. *Dowager Empress Cixi: The Woman Who Launched Modern China*. New York: Knopf, 2013.

Carlyon, Les. *The Great War*. Sydney: Pan Macmillan Australia, 2006.

Cole, E. Keith. *A History of the Church Missionary Society of Australia*. Melbourne: Church Missionary Society, 1971.

Cole, E. Keith. *Servants for Jesus' Sake: Long-serving Victorian CMS Missionaries*. Melbourne: Cole, 1993.

Crow, C. *Handbook for China*. Hong Kong: Kelly & Walsh, 1913, 1933.

Cunich, Peter "Deaconesses in the South China Mission of the Church Missionary Society (CMA), 1922–1951." In *Christian Women in Chinese Society: The Anglican Story*, edited by Wai Ching, Angela Wong, and Patricia C. K. Chiu, 85–106. Hong Kong: Hong Kong University Press, 2018.

Darley, Mary E. *The Light of the Morning: the Story of CEZMS work in the Kien-ning Prefecture of the Fuh-kien Province, China*. London: CEZMS, 1903.

Davin, Delta. "British Women Missionaries in Nineteenth-Century China." *Women's History Review* 1.2 (1992) 257–71. DOI: 10.1080/09612029200010204.

Dixson, Miriam. *The Real Matilda: Woman and Identity in Australia 1788 to the Present*. 3rd ed. Sydney: Penguin, 1984.

Drucker, A. R. "The Influence of Western Women in the Anti-Footbinding Movement, 1840–1911." In *Women in China: Current Directions in Historical Scholarship*, edited by Richard W. Guiso and Stanley Johannesen, 179–99. Youngstown, NY: Philo, 1981.

Dugdale-Pointon, T. D. P. "The Boxer Rebellion, 1900." *History of War*. 19 September 2004. Viewed 14 July 2012. www.history of war.org/article/wars-boxer.html.

Dukes, E. J. *Everyday Life in China or Scenes Along River and Road in Fuh-Kien*. London: Religious Tract Society, 1885.

BIBLIOGRAPHY

Dunch, Ryan. *Fuzhou Protestants and the Making of a Modern China 1857–1927*. New Haven: Yale University Press, 2001.

Dunlop, E. W. *Between Two Highways: A History of Early Croydon*. Sydney: Wentworth, 1969.

Edwards, E. H. *Fire and Sword in Shan-si: The Story of the Martyrdom of Foreigners and Chinese Christians*. London: Oliphant Anderson & Ferrier, 1906.

Faith-Davies, M. "Anti-Footbinding in Foochow City." *Women's Work in the Far East* 27 (1905) 116–19.

Fenby, Jonathan. *Chiang Kai Shek: China's Generalissimo and the Nation He Lost*. Lebanon IN: Di Capo, 2005.

———. *Modern China: The Fall and Rise of a Great Power, 1850 to the Present*. London: HarperCollins, 2008.

Fitzgerald, John. *Big White Lie: Chinese Australians in White Australia*. Sydney: UNSW, 2007.

Franklin, Miles. *Childhood at Brindabella*. Sydney: Angus & Robertson, 1963.

———. *My Brilliant Career*. Sydney: Angus & Robertson, 1901.

Garrett, S. *Social Reformers in Urban China: The Chinese YMCA*. Cambridge: Harvard University Press, 1970.

Glover, A. E. *A Thousand Miles of Miracles in China: A Personal Record of God's Delivering Power from the Hands of the Imperial Boxers of Shan-sai*. London: Hodder & Stoughton, 1904.

Goodlet, Ken. *Hazelbrook and Woodford: A Story of Two Blue Mountains Towns*. 2nd ed. Hazelbrook, NSW: Dayspring, 2011

Gray, N. "John Howe." In *Australian Dictionary of Biography*. Vol. 1. Melbourne: Melbourne University Press 1966.

Hague, William. *William Wilberforce: The Life of the Great Anti-Slave Trade Campaigner*. London: HarperPress, 2007.

Hammond, Thomas C. *The One Hundred Texts of the Irish Church Mission Society*. London: Society for Irish Church Missions, 1955.

Haskins, M. L. "God Knows." *The Desert*, private publication, 1908. (More popularly known as "The Gate of the Year.")

Hind, John. *Fukien Memories*. Belfast: James A. Nelson, 1951.

Hill, Ernestine. *The Territory: A Sprawling Saga of Australia's Tragic North*. Sydney: Angus & Robertson, 1951.

Hsu, I. C. Y. *The Rise of Modern China*. 5th ed. New York: Oxford University Press, 1995.

Jeremias, Joachim. *The Origins of Infant Baptism: A Further Study in Reply to Kurt Aland*. Translated by Dorothea A. Barton. 1963. Reprint, Eugene, OR: Wipf & Stock, 2004.

Johnstone, S. M. *The Australian Church Missionary Society: A Centenary History*. Sydney: CMS, 1942.

Jordan, Donald J. *The Northern Expedition: China's National Revolution of 1926–1928*. Honolulu: University of Hawaii Press, 1976.

Jowett, Philip. *The Armies of Warlord China 1911–1928*. Afglen, PA: Schiffer, 2014.

Judd, Stephen, and Ken Cable. *Sydney Anglicans: A History of the Diocese*. Sydney: Anglican Information Office, 1987.

Kinnear, Angus. *Against the Tide: The Story of Watchman Nee*. Fort Washington, PA: Christian Literature Crusade, 1992.

Kwok, Pui-Lan. *Chinese Women and Christianity 1860–1927*. American Academy of Religion Academy Series 75. Atlanta: Scholars, 1992.

BIBLIOGRAPHY

Lamb, Margaret. *Going It Alone: Mary Andrews—Missionary to China 1938-1951*. Sydney: Aquila, 1995.
Lambert, Tony. *China's Christian Millions*. Rev. ed. Abingdon: Monarch, 2006.
Lambert, L. T. *A History of the Parish of Lawson 1842-1971*. Greenacre, NSW: Gowan, 1972.
Lary, Diana. *China's Republic*. Cambridge: Cambridge University Press, 2007.
Latourette Kenneth S. *The Chinese: Their History and Culture*. 3rd ed. New York: MacMillan, 1936.
Lea-Scarlett, E. *Queanbeyan: District and People*. Queanbeyan, NSW: Queanbeyan Municipal Council, 1968.
Lee, Joseph Tse-Hei. *The Bible and the Gun: Christianity in South China 1860-1900*. East Asia. New York: Routledge, 2002.
Li, L. "Christian Women's Education in China in the 19th and Early 20th Centuries." Salem State 20 March 2012. www4.samford.edu/lillyhumanrights/papers/Li_Christian.pdf, 1-13/ s.
Lin, J. "In the Shadow of Watchman Nee: The Life of the Rev. Lin Pu-chi." Learning from the Past, Looking to the Future, Hong Kong Sheng Kung Hui International Academic Conference, 7 June 2012.
Linder, Robert D. *The Long Tragedy: Australian Evangelicals and the Great War, 1914-1918*. Adelaide: Open Book, 2000.
Loane, Marcus L. *Archbishop Mowll: The Biography of Howard Kilverton Mowll, Archbishop of Sydney and Primate of Australia*. London: Hodder & Stoughton, 1960.
———. "Dorothy Ann Mowll." In *Australian Dictionary of Evangelical Biography*. Edited by Brian Dickey. Sydney: Evangelical History Association, 1994.
Lodwick, Kenneth L. *Crusaders Against Opium: Protestant Missionaries in China, 1874-1917*. Lexington: University of Kentucky Press, 1996.
Lovell, J. *The Opium War: Drugs, Dreams and the Making of China*. Sydney: Picador, 2011.
Manne, Robert. *Hamilton Hume: Our Greatest Explorer*. Sydney: Hachette, 2017.
McDonald Jr., Angus W. *The Urban Origins of Rural Revolution: Elites and the Masses in Hunan Province, China, 1911-1927*, Berkeley: University of California Press, 1978.
Millard, E. C. *The Same Lord: An Account of the Mission Tour of the Rev. George Grubb M.A. in Australia, Tasmania and New Zealand from April 3rd 1891 to July 7th 1892*, London: Marlborough, 1893.
Murray, Andrew. *The Holiest of All*. New York: Randolph, 1894.
Norris, F. L. *China, Handbooks of English Church Expansion*. Mowbray, London, 1908.
O'Brien, Anne. *God's Willing Workers: Women and Religion in Australia*. Sydney: UNSW Press, 2005.
O'Neill, Mark. *The Chinese Labour Corps: The Forgotten Chinese Labourers of the First World War*. London: Penguin, 2014
Pakula, H. *The Last Empress: Madame Chang Kai-Shek and the Birth of Modern China*. New York: Simon & Schuster, 2009.
Pearson, Charles H. *National Life and Character: A Forecast*. London: MacMillan, 1893.
Peterson, E. "Sophia Sackville Newton." In *150th Anniversary St Luke's Burwood with Concord*, 22-23. Sydney: St. Luke's Burwood, 2009.
Phillips, Walter. *Defending 'A Christian Country': Churchmen and Society in New South Wales in the 1880's and After*. Brisbane: Queensland University Press, 1981.
Pitcher, P. W. *A Sketch of Kuliang Mountains and Environments*. 2nd ed. Foochow: Methodist Publishing House, 1907.

BIBLIOGRAPHY

Pierson, A. T. *The Keswick Movement in Precepts and Practice*. New York: Funk & Wagnalls, 1903.

Pixley, N. S. "John Dight and His Descendants." *Royal Historical Society of Queensland* 22 (1977) 10–20.

Preston, Diana. *The Boxer Rebellion: The Dramatic Story of China's War on Foreigners That Shook the World in the Summer of 1900*. New York: Walker, 1999.

Rawlinson, F., ed. *The China Mission Year Book 1924*. Shanghai: Christian Literature Society, 1924.

Roberts, Dana. *Understanding Watchman Nee*. Plainfield, NJ: Haven, 1980.

Rose, M. "Formal Women's Ministry: The Deaconess." In *Freedom from Sanctified Sexism — Women Transforming the Church*, 56–75. McGregor, QLD: Allira, 1996.

Rowden, Harold H. "The Concept of Living by Faith." In *Mission and Meaning: Essays Presented to Peter Cotterell*, edited by Anthony Billington et al., 339–56. Carlisle, UK: Paternoster, 1995.

Rowland, E. C. *A Century of the English Church in New South Wales*. Sydney: Angus & Robertson, 1948.

Schiffrin, Harold S. *Sun Yat-Sen and the Origins of the Chinese Revolution*. Los Angeles: University of California Press, 2010.

Severn, Joan. *The Teston Story: Kent Village Life through the Ages*. Teston: Rufus Fay, 1975.

Slater, Frances. *The Wolfe Sisters of Foochow, China: Born to Evangelise*. Self-published with John Fitzgerald. 2017.

Smith, Arthur H. *Village Life in China: A Study in Sociology*. New York: Revell, 1899.

"St Paul's Church Woodford." *Church of England Historical Society*, 1 September 1970, 60–63.

Stead, W. T., ed. "Imperilled Missionaries in China." *Review of Reviews* (1900) 4–5.

Steele, J. *Early Days of Windsor N. S. Wales*. Sydney: Tyrell's, 1916.

Stock, Eugene. *For Christ and Fuh-kien: The Story of the Fuh-kien Mission of the Church Missionary Society*. London: Church Missionary Society, 1904.

———. *A History of the Church Missionary Society*. Vol. 4. London: Church Missionary Society, 1916.

Taylor, Howard, and Mrs H. *Hudson Taylor and the China Inland Mission*. Vol. 2: *The Growth of a Work of God*. London: China Inland Mission, 1918.

Taylor Jay. *The Generalissimo: Chiang Kai-Shek and the Struggle for Modern China*. Cambridge, MA: Belknap, 2011.

Ten, George Soo (1848–1934), *Australian Dictionary of Biography*, vol. 6, 1976 at the National Centre of Biography, Australian National University, https://adb.anu.edu.au/biography/ten-george-soo-hoo-4699/text778/

Tess, Nora. *Caught for Life: A Story of the Anglican Deaconess Order in Australia*. Araluen: Nora Tess, 1993.

Thompson, P. *Shanghai Fury: Australian Heroes of Revolutionary China*. Sydney: Heinemann, 2011.

Twain, Mark. *Mark Twain in Australia and New Zealand*. 1897. Reprint, London: Penguin, 1973.

The Unfinished Task of China and Japan. Sydney: CMS, 1938.

Wasserman, Jeffrey N. *Student Protests in Twentieth-Century China: The View from Shanghai*. Stanford: Stanford University Press, 1991.

Webster, R. H. *Currency Lad: The Story of Hamilton Hume and the Explorers*. Sydney: Leisure Magazines, 1982.

BIBLIOGRAPHY

Welch, Ian. "Nellie, Topsy and Annie: Anglican Martyrs, Fujian Province, China, 1 August, 1895." Paper Presented to the First Tasmanian Missionary Conference on Australia and New Zealand Missionaries, Australian National University, Canberra ACT, 8–10 October 2004.

———. "Women's Work for Women: Women Missionaries in 19th century China." Paper presented to the 8th Women in Asia Conference, University of Technology, Sydney, 26–28 October 2005.

West, Janet. "The Role of the Woman Missionary, 1880–1914." *Lucas* 21 & 22 (1996) 31–46.

Willard, Myra. *History of the White Australia Policy to 1920*. University of Melbourne Publications 1. Melbourne: Melbourne University Press, 1923.

Wise, Bernard. *The Making of the Australian Commonwealth*. London: Longmans, Green, 1913.

Yu Pa-ching, "Chinese Seamen in London and St. Helena in the Nineteenth Century." In *Law, Labour and Empire: Comparative Perspectives on Seafarers, c. 1500–1800*, edited by Maria Fusaro et al., 287–303. London: Palgrave MacMillan. https://doi.org/10.1057/9781137447463_16)/.

www.ingramcontent.com/pod-product-compliance
Lightning Source LLC
Chambersburg PA
CBHW050818160426
43192CB00010B/1813